Editorial Project Manager
Erica N. Russikoff, M.A.

Editor in Chief
Brent L. Fox, M. Ed.

Creative Director
Sarah M. Fournier

Cover Artist
Diem Pascarella

Art Coordinator & Illustrator
Renée Mc Elwee

Imaging
Crystal-Dawn Keitz

Publisher
Mary D. Smith, M.S. Ed.

For standards correlations, please visit *http://www.teachercreated.com/standards/*.

Author
Tracy Edmunds, M.A. Ed.

Teacher Created Resources
12621 Western Avenue
Garden Grove, CA 92841
www.teachercreated.com
ISBN: 978-1-4206-8274-8
©2021 Teacher Created Resources
Reprinted, 2022
Made in U.S.A.

TABLE OF CONTENTS

INTRODUCTION

This book will help you implement engineering design challenges in your classroom by using stories as an entry point. This interdisciplinary approach helps students contextualize engineering and design concepts, and they will get excited about engineering!

The stories are fun and engaging and have been specifically developed to include several problems—some obvious and some not so obvious. Students read a story and look for and discuss the problems they find, which encourages them to reread and analyze the text of the story. Once students have chosen a problem, they work in teams to define what they need to create to solve it. Teams then use the engineering design process to plan, build, test, and improve their solution using recycled materials and common supplies. Finally, students reflect on their experience through writing. This integration of literacy and STEM allows students to acquire and practice skills in both areas.

Engineering challenges may be different from what you and your students are used to. Instead of lecturing or demonstrating, you will be putting materials in the hands of students, setting them up for success, and turning them loose to create and build. You become a facilitator—scaffolding when necessary; providing guidance; and checking in with groups to offer encouragement, advice, correction, and support. Motivate students to help one another, both within teams and between teams.

There may be a bit of a learning curve at first, but once students understand how engineering challenges work, they really dive into them. They become fully engaged in working together on their own terms, manipulating materials, and solving a compelling problem, with their hands and minds occupied and on task. And these challenges are not conducive to silence; a low buzz of purposeful conversation indicates that students are actively engaged. Your biggest problem may be getting them to wrap things up!

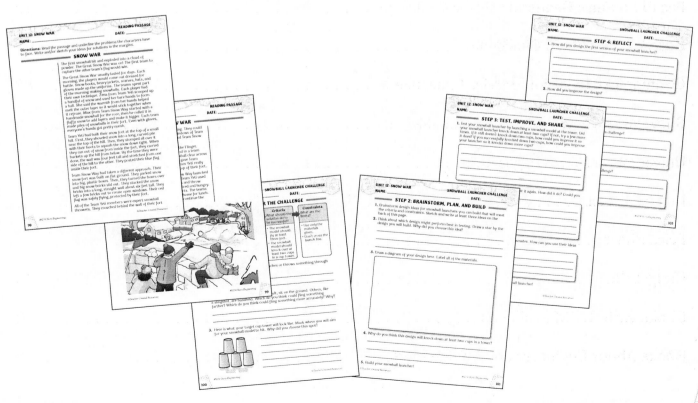

READ THE STORY AND IDENTIFY PROBLEMS

Each unit in this book features an original, leveled short story to engage students and provide context for engineering problems. After students read a story, have them identify some of the multiple problems embedded within. For your reference, the teacher section of each unit lists some problems within the story and possible engineering challenges to solve them. Students may identify even more problems within a story or create problems and challenges based on what they've read.

GUIDED CHALLENGES

For each story, one specific problem has been selected for a guided challenge. The challenge is predefined through criteria and constraints, and challenge pages support student teams as they work through the engineering design process to solve it. These scaffolded challenges can help students work through the process of creating a solution, even if they have not participated in an engineering challenge before. The guided challenges have been created with small groups of two to five students in mind, but they can certainly be solved by students working alone.

Step 1: *Prepare for the Challenge* defines the criteria and constraints and gives students a task that will help them prepare to solve the challenge.

Step 2: *Brainstorm, Plan, and Build* leads students in brainstorming ideas for their solutions, identifying the best ideas, creating a diagram or plan of their solution, and choosing materials.

Step 3: *Test, Improve, and Share* prompts students to test and refine their solution and collaborate with other teams to identify areas of improvement.

Step 4: *Reflect* asks students to evaluate both their final solution and the process of planning and building it.

STUDENT-DEFINED CHALLENGES

Once students are comfortable with the engineering design process, the *Universal Challenge Pages* (pages 104–107) give them some structure for tackling problems they identify on their own. They define a problem by identifying criteria and constraints using context from the story, and work through the engineering design process to create solutions.

CRITERIA AND CONSTRAINTS

Every engineering challenge starts with criteria and constraints that student engineers must follow.

- *Criteria* are things the solution needs to have or do to be successful or the requirements that must be met.
- *Constraints* are limitations placed on the solution.

When planning, testing, and evaluating a solution, students should continually think about how it fulfills the criteria and follows the constraints.

CRITERIA AND CONSTRAINTS (CONT.)

In the guided challenges, the criteria and constraints are given. When students take on their own challenges using the *Universal Challenge Pages*, the first thing they must do is define the initial criteria and constraints.

If students ask, "Can I do this?" refer them back to the criteria and constraints to check for themselves. Criteria and constraints create an envelope within which students can be creative, so try to give them as much freedom as possible within it. If students levy a charge of "cheating" at a new idea, have a group discussion about the criteria and constraints and whether the new idea falls within them.

Of course, don't hesitate to add constraints if necessary. "Can I throw this across the room?" or "Is it okay to light this on fire?" most definitely call for new constraints! The challenges give students a certain amount of freedom, but they should not be free-for-alls.

NO "RIGHT" ANSWERS

Engineering challenges can have many solutions, so don't try to predict or prescribe what students will produce. Students will surprise you with solutions you might never have considered.

Students often need help reframing failure as a necessary part of the engineering design process. Failure is not the end of an engineering project; it is a positive step along the way to discovering and designing solutions. Review the *Engineering Design Process* (page 7) frequently, pointing out that the test-and-improve cycle is all about looking at why failure happens and how to fix it.

Not every solution has to be successful within the time available, as long as students go through the entire engineering design process and can explain how their solution addresses (or misses) the criteria and constraints.

RECORDING

In the real world, engineers do a lot of writing. They write procedures, reports, funding requests, and more. And they write not only to communicate with others, but also to clarify their thinking, to explore new ideas, and to come to conclusions. As part of the engineering challenges in this book, students will record their planning, testing, and refining of their designs on paper. At the end of each challenge, they will evaluate and write about their experience by answering reflection questions.

Both speaking and writing give students an opportunity to articulate their thinking. As they work on a challenge, they discuss their work with other students. These discussions allow students to work out their thoughts and observations aloud, which makes writing easier. This is particularly helpful for English language learners who practice vocabulary and sentence structure as a natural part of their challenge work time. Encourage students to use their natural language during challenges to communicate their ideas—even if their grammar isn't perfect. When assessing students' writing for these challenges, don't worry so much about spelling and punctuation—focus on the ideas.

RECORDING (CONT.)

Visual and symbolic representations such as diagrams, blueprints, technical drawings, schematics, and models are integral parts of engineering. In every challenge, students are asked to sketch and label their ideas. Sketching helps students get their ideas on paper quickly and encourages them to think through the relationships of the parts to one another and to the whole. Drawings are also useful for assessment, as you can see how well students understood the challenge concepts by how they represent those concepts visually.

ASSESSMENT

As students work through the challenges, check for understanding through formative assessment by examining the following evidence:

- Observations of and discussions with students during work time
- Class sharing and discussions
- Written and drawn responses on challenge pages

These formative assessments provide multiple sources of evidence to guide you in making inferences about what students understand and are capable of doing and also point toward next steps in instruction.

For summative assessment, you may want to have individual students complete the *Step 4: Reflect* page for each challenge.

MATERIALS

The challenges in this book call for recycled materials, along with classroom supplies you probably already have. For most of the challenges, the materials lists are suggestions—you can use whatever materials you have available. See page 108 for more information about materials.

TIPS FOR MATERIALS

- Develop specific routines for how students will access materials, and practice with them before each activity. Also, be sure to review safe practices with items like scissors and pushpins.
- Make clear which materials students can alter (cut, fold, etc.) and which are non-alterable materials. You don't want students to break rulers and cut apart textbooks!
- You can vary the challenges by varying the available materials. Restricting the number of available materials forces students to think creatively to use them in new ways. Offering a wide selection of materials means they will have to think critically about what they really need.

BUDGETS

To add an extra layer to each challenge—and some more math—assign prices to materials and give students a budget for their projects. Materials that are in short supply or that are of easier use in solving the challenges can have higher prices. Fill out the *Price Sheet* (page 109), and give students a copy of that and the *Budget Sheet* (page 110).

Identify Problem

↓

Brainstorm

↓

Design

↓

Build

Redesign

Test & Evaluate

↓

Share Solution

PLOT SUMMARY:

Sid and Ruby want to play kickball, but they don't have a ball. They make a ball by upcycling plastic shopping bags and string. It's so successful that they decide to make more upcycled toys.

UPCYCLED GAME CHALLENGE:

Problem What problem will you solve?	Challenge What will you do?	Criteria What should the solution do to be successful?	Constraints What are the limits?
Sid, Ruby, and Sky want to make more toys.	Design and build a quick, active game using upcycled materials.	• The game should include movement of some kind. • The game should be playable by one to four players. • The game should be quick to play (two minutes or less).	• Use only upcycled materials. • Must run on kid power; no batteries or electricity.

OTHER POSSIBLE PROBLEMS AND CHALLENGES:

Students can use the *Universal Challenge Pages* (pages 104–107) to create solutions to any of the problems below or problems they identify themselves.

Problem	The plastic-bag jump rope with duct-tape handles is hard to turn.
Possible Challenge	• Design a jump rope with better handles that is easy to turn.

Problem	The kids' plastic-bag ball doesn't bounce as well as a red rubber ball.
Possible Challenge	• Design a ball made from recycled materials that bounces well.

Problem	The kids want to make lots of different toys.
Possible Challenges	• Engineer outdoor toys from recycled materials (e.g., tetherball, wagon, kite). • Engineer indoor toys from recycled materials (e.g., board games, card games, toy cars, action figures, building blocks, musical instruments).

MATERIALS:

> **Suggested:** any clean, nonhazardous, used materials such as scratch paper, empty food containers and lids, cardboard boxes, plastic bottles and caps, wood scraps, paint, rubber bands; connecting materials such as glue, tape, staples, string (For this challenge, the more materials you can offer, the better!)

LESSON PLAN:

1. Have students read the passage and discuss the problems they identified. Use these questions as prompts:

   - What toys do you like to play with?
   - Have you ever made your own toys? What did you make? How did you make it?
   - Did the kids in the story have any problems while they were making toys? How did they solve their problems?

2. Discuss the term *upcycled* with students. It means using materials that would otherwise be discarded (e.g., trash, recycling) to make something new. Examples might include using an empty plastic jar to hold pencils and pens or stretching a balloon over it to make a drum. Some people call this turning trash into treasure!

3. Introduce the Upcycled Game Challenge by reading through the challenge pages together. Show students the available materials and review the criteria and constraints. At first, students will think about active games that are played by moving something. If they have trouble thinking of examples, prompt them to think of carnival games or "minute to win it"-type games.

4. Give students time to prepare, brainstorm, plan, and build their games. Circulate to observe and answer questions as students work on their solutions. Remind them to use the challenge pages to guide them as they work through the engineering design process.

5. Students should have peers play-test their games and give feedback, then revise their designs and test again.

6. When students have completed the challenge, have them demonstrate and explain their upcycled game to the class. If desired, you could have a game day when students play one another's games.

7. Have students fill out the reflection page.

8. If time, allow students to choose their own problem and testing setup and use the *Universal Challenge Pages* (pages 104–107) to complete their challenge.

Directions: Read the passage and underline the problems the characters have to face. Write and/or sketch your ideas for solutions in the margins.

LET'S MAKE TOYS

Sid and Ruby were sitting on Sid's front steps, trying to think of something fun to do.

"Let's play kickball," suggested Sid.

"We don't have a ball," answered Ruby.

Sid thought for a minute. "We could make our own," he said.

"Really? How?" asked Ruby.

Sid took Ruby into his kitchen. He pulled out a box of plastic shopping bags. "My mom saves these for recycling. She won't mind if we use them." Then he got a spool of string and some scissors. He squished up a plastic bag into a small ball. Then he wrapped another bag around it.

"Oh, I get it!" said Ruby. She wrapped another plastic bag around the still-forming ball.

Once they had added enough plastic bags to make the ball about the size of a red rubber kickball, Sid grabbed the spool of string. He wrapped string around the plastic-bag ball in different directions. He kept wrapping until the plastic bags stayed together all around the ball. Finally, he tied the string and cut off the end.

Sid and Ruby ran out to the sidewalk. They kicked the ball back and forth a few times.

"Hey, this works pretty well," said Ruby. "It's not bouncy like a kickball, but it rolls okay."

They knocked on their friends' doors and asked everyone to come out and play. They had a fun game of kickball with their friends until it got dark.

The next day, Ruby asked Sid, "Can we make any other things to play with?"

LET'S MAKE TOYS

"Hmmm," said Sid. "Let's make a list of toys we like and then we can think about which ones we could make."

Their list included outdoor toys like a tetherball, roller skates, a wagon, a kite, and a jump rope. They also listed indoor toys like video games, board games, card games, toy cars, action figures, building blocks, and musical instruments. As they looked over the list, they decided that it would be too hard to make their own video game or roller skates, but they could probably make any of the other toys on the list. The only problem was that they wouldn't have time to make them all!

First, they tied a long piece of rope onto their plastic-bag kickball. They tied the other end of the rope to a lamppost and made a tetherball out of it! Ruby had an idea for making a jump rope. She asked Sid for more plastic bags and some scissors. She showed him how to cut the bags into strips and braid them. They braided together a lot of strips until they had a rope long enough to use for a jump rope. Sid wrapped duct tape around each end for a handle. They asked their friend Sky to help them make a second jump rope. Then they all jumped double-dutch. It was fun, even if it was kind of hard to turn the ropes with duct-tape handles.

After lunch, Sid, Ruby, and Sky wanted to play inside. They decided to make their own board game. Sid got a cereal box, and they cut it open so it would lie flat. They sketched out the game on the cardboard in pencil and then filled it in with markers. They used some of Sky's mom's buttons for game pieces, and they made cards by writing on index cards. Their game was sort of a mix of a trivia game and checkers. They couldn't decide whether to call it "Checkia" or "Trivers." It was so much fun that they wanted to make more games and toys, but it was time for Sky and Ruby to go home.

STEP 1: PREPARE FOR THE CHALLENGE

Problem	Challenge	Criteria	Constraints
What problem will you solve?	What will you do?	What should the solution do to be successful?	What are the limits?
Sid, Ruby, and Sky want to make more toys.	Design and build a quick, active game using upcycled materials.	• The game should include movement of some kind. • The game should be playable by one to four players. • The game should be quick to play (two minutes or less).	• Use only upcycled materials. • Must run on kid power; no batteries or electricity.

Directions: Make a quick, active game from upcycled materials. Your game must include movement of some kind and must use kid power (no batteries or electricity). No board games—your game must be active!

Think of games you have played in which you must move something. For example, the kids in the story played kickball in which they **kicked** a ball. When they played tetherball, they **hit** or **pushed** the ball. Your game can be an indoor or outdoor game.

Write three examples of games below as well as the movement or movements that you use to play each game. Here are some examples of movements: push, pull, throw, kick, hit, roll, turn, twist, swing, and balance.

Game	Movement(s)

STEP 2: BRAINSTORM, PLAN, AND BUILD

1. Brainstorm design ideas for upcycled games you can create that will meet the criteria and constraints. Sketch and write at least three ideas on the back of this page.

2. To test your game, you will ask other kids to play it. Your game should not be too hard to win, but not too easy, either! Think about which design might perform best in testing. Draw a star by the design you will build. Why did you choose this idea?

_____

_____

_____

3. Draw a diagram of your design here. Label all of the materials.

4. Why do you think this game design is the best one?

_____

_____

_____

5. Make your upcycled game!

STEP 3: TEST, IMPROVE, AND SHARE

1. Check to see that your game meets each criteria and constraint:

☐ The game is made from upcycled materials.

☐ The game includes movement of some kind.

☐ The game can be played by one to four players.

☐ The game is quick to play (two minutes or less).

☐ The game uses kid power (no batteries or electricity).

2. Does your game design meet all the criteria? If not, how could you improve it?

_____

_____

_____

3. Ask some classmates to play your game. They must be able to understand how to play, so you may want to write some directions. After they play, ask them to answer these questions:

• Did you understand how to play the game? _____

• Was the game too hard or too easy? Explain. _____

_____

• Did you enjoy playing the game? _____

• Do you have any suggestions to make the game better? If so, what are they?

_____

_____

4. How can you use your classmates' ideas to make your game better?

_____

_____

_____

5. Keep testing and improving your upcycled game!

STEP 4: REFLECT

1. How did you design the first version of your upcycled game?

2. How did you improve the design?

3. What was the hardest part about this challenge?

4. What have you learned from this challenge?

PLOT SUMMARY:

Natia, who is stranded on a tropical beach, works to survive.

MODEL SHELTER CHALLENGE:

Problem	Challenge	Criteria	Constraints
What problem will you solve?	What will you do?	What should the solution do to be successful?	What are the limits?
Natia needs a better shelter.	Design and build a model shelter for Natia.	• The shelter should keep out the rain and sun. • The shelter should include a comfortable place to sleep (bed, blanket, pillow). • The shelter should have a place to store food where it won't get wet or sandy.	Use only the materials given.

OTHER POSSIBLE PROBLEMS AND CHALLENGES:

Students can use the *Universal Challenge Pages* (pages 104–107) to create solutions to any of the problems below or problems they identify themselves.

Problem	Natia needs food.
Possible Challenges	• Design a reliable way to catch fish. • Design a way to reach and pick fruit high in a tree.

Problem	Natia caught some crabs, but she has no way to cook them.
Possible Challenge	• Design a solar cooker.

Problem	Natia needs more fresh water.
Possible Challenge	• Design a way to catch and store rainwater.

MATERIALS:

Suggested: a wide selection of natural materials such as sticks, leaves, stems, and rocks in a variety of sizes and shapes

PREPARATION:

The difficulty of this challenge depends on the materials available. Ideally, offer only natural materials. If necessary, substitute materials such as straws and craft sticks for natural sticks. Do not include tape or staplers—challenge students to use natural materials such as leaves and stems as connectors. If you want to make the challenge slightly easier, provide string. While students will not be testing their designs in this project, you will need a space for them to display their model shelters so that everyone can examine them and give feedback.

LESSON PLAN:

1. Have students read the passage and discuss the problems they identified. Use these questions as prompts:

   - Where do you think Natia is? How do you think she got there?
   - How do you think you would feel if you were stranded alone?
   - What challenges does Natia have? Did she solve any of them? How?

2. Introduce the Model Shelter Challenge by reading through the challenge pages together. Explain to students that they will be creating a model of a shelter. A *model* is a small copy of something, like a model airplane or a model of the human heart. Let students know that for this challenge they won't be testing their designs. They will design and build their model shelter to meet three criteria, or requirements.

3. Show students the available materials and review the criteria and constraint. Give them time to think about the materials and complete the tasks for Step 1 (page 20). This will help them think through their materials choices.

4. Give students time to prepare, brainstorm, plan, and build their model shelters. Let them know that as long as they meet the criteria, they can add any extra features they want to their shelters, such as chairs, a table, or flags and decorations. Circulate to observe and answer questions as students work on their solutions. Remind them to use the challenge pages to guide them as they work through the engineering design process.

5. Have students evaluate their model shelters by checking them against the criteria. Allow time for students to share their solutions with the class and get feedback from peers. Then they should revise and improve their designs.

6. When students have completed the challenge, have them show and explain their model shelters to the class. Then have them fill out the reflection page.

7. If time, allow students to choose their own problem and testing setup and use the *Universal Challenge Pages* (pages 104–107) to complete their challenge.

Directions: Read the passage and underline the problems the character has to face. Write and/or sketch your ideas for solutions in the margins.

═══ STRANDED ═══

Natia stood perfectly still in the ankle-deep water. She didn't dare move a muscle. Slowly, the fish began to swim out from their hiding places under the rocks. When one of the bigger fish came close enough, she struck as fast as lightning. Her sharpened stick narrowly missed, and the fish disappeared. "Looks like seaweed for dinner again," she thought. She stepped carefully over the sharp rocks that formed the tide pools and headed back to the beach. Too bad her shoes had floated away when she didn't pay attention to how high the tide was getting.

She walked up the beach and flopped down under her lean-to, exhausted. As huge raindrops started to fall, she was thankful that she had added extra leaves to the roof. She cracked a coconut against a rock and set both halves out to catch some water. Watching the rain, she thought about how she could capture more of the water to use later. While it rained, she worked on building her crab trap.

When it got dark, Natia stretched out on the sand floor of the lean-to. She had piled up some leaves to make a pillow, but she had to keep gathering them back together. To keep warm, she buried her body a little way under the sand.

The rain finally stopped early the next morning. Natia was feeling brave—and hungry—so she ventured farther away from the beach and into the rain forest. She saw some parrots eating small, red fruits high up in a tree. The birds were very messy eaters! Natia picked up a piece of fruit that the birds dropped and tasted it. It was very sweet! She gathered up the uneaten fruits she could find on the ground and carried them back to her lean-to. She ate about a third of them and set the rest aside for later.

STRANDED

She spent the afternoon setting her crab trap and gathering seaweed at the tide pools. The sun beat down mercilessly. She was lucky that her T-shirt and shorts were holding up well, with just a few small rips and holes. It was just a shame she didn't have a hat. When she checked the crab trap, she was delighted to find two good-sized crabs! Then she realized that she didn't have a way to cook them. Raw crab did not sound good. So she let them go back into the tide pools.

After a dinner of sandy fruit and seaweed, she turned her attention to rescue. Building a raft was not an option because she didn't have any tools. A message in a bottle wouldn't work because she didn't have a bottle. She knew if she could write SOS in huge letters on the beach, there was a chance a passing ship or plane would see it. But what could she use to make the letters? Leaves would probably blow away. Rocks would work, but she didn't see enough on the beach to make the letters very big. Maybe there were more rocks farther into the rain forest. As she drifted off to sleep, Natia made a mental note to go rock hunting in the morning.

STEP 1: PREPARE FOR THE CHALLENGE

Problem	Challenge	Criteria	Constraints
What problem will you solve?	**What will you do?**	**What should the solution do to be successful?**	**What are the limits?**
Natia needs a better shelter.	Design and build a model shelter for Natia.	• The shelter should keep out the rain and sun. • The shelter should include a comfortable place to sleep (bed, blanket, pillow). • The shelter should have a place to store food where it won't get wet or sandy.	Use only the materials given.

1. Shelters can be built many different ways. Below are some examples of simple shelters. Think about what Natia's shelter needs to do and what shape might work best to meet the criteria. Could you combine ideas or create a new shape? Sketch ideas on the back of this page.

Lean-to   **Thatched Dome Hut**   **Teepee**   **Ramada**

2. Because Natia is stranded without tools, she will have to put her shelter together without nails, screws, or bolts. Think about ways to use the available materials to keep the structural pieces of the shelter attached to one another so it doesn't fall down.

STEP 2: BRAINSTORM, PLAN, AND BUILD

1. Brainstorm design ideas to meet the criteria and constraint. Sketch and write at least three ideas for each criteria.

Keeps out the rain and sun	Includes a comfortable place to sleep (bed, blanket, pillow)	Has a place to store food where it won't get wet or sandy

2. Think about which ideas might work best. Circle the idea you will use for each criteria. Why did you choose these ideas?

_____

_____

_____

3. Combine your ideas and draw a diagram of your model shelter design here. Once you have met the criteria, you can add as many extra features as you want. Label all of the materials.

4. Build your model shelter!

STEP 3: TEST, IMPROVE, AND SHARE

1. Check to see that your model shelter meets each criteria:

☐ Keeps out rain and sun

☐ Has a comfortable place to sleep

☐ Has a place to store food

2. Does your model shelter meet all the criteria? If not, how could you improve it?

_____

_____

_____

_____

_____

3. Share your model shelter with classmates. How can you use their ideas to make it better?

_____

_____

_____

_____

_____

4. Keep redesigning until your model shelter meets the criteria!

STEP 4: REFLECT

1. How does your design meet each criteria?

Keeps out rain and sun: _____

Has a comfortable place to sleep: _____

Has a place to store food: _____

2. How did you improve your design?

_____

_____

_____

3. What extra features did you add to your shelter?

_____

_____

4. What was the hardest part about this challenge?

_____

_____

5. What have you learned from this challenge?

_____

_____

PLOT SUMMARY:

Hamsters Miss Cookie Cheeks and Sir Fluffsalot go on a quest for a carrot treasure.

HAMSTER SLIDE CHALLENGE:

Problem What problem will you solve?	Challenge What will you do?	Criteria What should the solution do to be successful?	Constraints What are the limits?
The hamsters need to get from the top of the dresser to the floor quickly and safely.	Build a slide for the hamsters and give them a safe landing.	• The hamster model (three interlocking math manipulative cubes) should slide smoothly down from the starting level to the floor. • There should be a soft landing at the bottom of the slide.	• Use only the materials given. • The hamster model can't slip off the sides of the slide.

OTHER POSSIBLE PROBLEMS AND CHALLENGES:

Students can use the *Universal Challenge Pages* (pages 104–107) to create solutions to any of the problems below or problems they identify themselves.

Problem	It is hard for the hamsters to walk across the pile of laundry.
Possible Challenges	• Build special shoes for the hamsters that work like snowshoes, distributing their weight to make walking easier. • Build stilts for the hamsters. • Create a tunneling machine so they can go under the pile.

Problem	The hamsters need help getting the carrot back to their cage.
Possible Challenges	• Build a carrier with wheels to help them move the carrot. • Engineer a device using pulleys to help them get the carrot up to the top of the dresser. • Build a catapult to launch the carrot up to the cage.

MATERIALS:

Required: snap-together blocks (e.g., Unifix cubes, Snap Cubes, Legos)

Suggested: structural materials such as different kinds of paper and cardboard, paper towel and toilet paper rolls, assorted containers; different materials for the surface of the slide, such as fabrics, foil, plastic wrap; soft or squishy materials for the landing, such as cotton balls or batting, bubble wrap; connectors such as clothes pins, binder clips, rubber bands, tape

PREPARATION:

Designate a starting level for testing, such as a chair, desk, or table. You can make the challenge easier by using a lower surface, such as the bottom shelf of a bookcase, or make it more difficult by using a higher surface, such as the top of a cabinet. Snap three identical blocks together to create a hamster model to show students.

LESSON PLAN:

1. Have students read the passage and discuss the problems they identified. Use these questions as prompts:

    - What do you know about hamsters? Do you have one? Have you seen one?
    - What problems did the hamsters have in trying to get the carrot?
    - Did the hamsters solve any of their problems? How did they solve them?
    - Can you think of better solutions to the hamsters' problems?

2. Introduce the Hamster Slide Challenge by reading through the challenge pages together. Show students the available materials and review the criteria and constraints. Show students the hamster model you created with snap-together blocks and warn them that they should NEVER use real animals in any situation that could be dangerous. Explain that the three-block hamster models will be the same for every team to make testing fair.

3. Give students time to prepare, brainstorm, plan, and build their hamster slides. Circulate to observe and answer questions as students work on their solutions. Remind them to use the challenge pages to guide them as they work through the engineering design process. When they are ready for testing, observe to ensure fair and equal testing conditions for each student or team.

4. Have students share their solutions with the class and get feedback from peers, then revise their designs and test again.

5. When students have completed the challenge, have them demonstrate and explain their hamster slides to the class. Then have them fill out the reflection page.

6. If time, allow students to choose their own problem and testing setup and use the *Universal Challenge Pages* (pages 104–107) to complete their challenge.

NAME: _____   DATE: _____

Directions: Read the passage and underline the problems the characters have to face. Write and/or sketch your ideas for solutions in the margins.

A TASTY MISSION

Sir Fluffsalot and Miss Cookie Cheeks looked out over the landscape of Sam's room. They could see the carrot lying abandoned on the floor near the bed.

"What a tasty treasure," said Fluffsalot as he smacked his lips. "Is there any way we can get to it?"

Cheeks scratched her ear and thought. "We'll have to get out of this cage, down to the ground, and across the mountain of laundry. Then we'll need to find a way to get the carrot back up here."

"Well, first things first," said Fluffsalot. "How do we escape from here? I don't know how to open the door."

"That roof doesn't look to be attached too tightly," said Cheeks. She shimmied up the bars and poked her nose through a space at the top of the cage. "If I can just...oof!" She pushed her head up against the roof, and *POP!* The top of the cage lifted, and she clambered out and down the bars. Fluffsalot wasn't far behind.

As they stood on the edge of the dresser and looked down, they realized they couldn't jump without getting hurt. Cheeks noticed that the back of the dresser was close to the curtains. She jumped onto the curtains, and as she climbed backwards down to the floor, Fluffsalot was right behind her.

Now, they faced a pile of dirty clothes that stretched from the bed to the closet, with no way to go around. The hamsters would just have to go over it. As they stepped onto the mountain of shirts and jeans, it sank beneath them. "This is like walking in deep snow," said Cheeks. By the time they reached the other side of the pile, they were exhausted. As they sat, panting, Flufflsalot suddenly let out an excited squeak. "Look!" he exclaimed. The carrot was close enough to touch, and it was longer than either of them.

"How on Earth will we get it back home?" cried Fluffsalot.

A TASTY MISSION

"Well, we could just eat it here," suggested Cheeks.

"If I eat all that, I'll be too heavy to make it back over the mountain and up the curtains," sighed Fluffsalot. "But a small taste won't hurt!" He bit into the tasty, orange goodness.

Then they heard the front door slam, followed by footsteps pounding up the stairs. As Sam burst into the room, the two hamsters froze. At first, Sam didn't notice them. She threw her backpack on the desk and ran back down the stairs.

"That was close," warned Fluffsalot. "She'll be back."

"What should we do?" worried Cheeks.

Fluffsalot sank his teeth into the end of the carrot and pulled, but it wouldn't budge. "Mcome mhelp mme," he mumbled. Both hamsters bit and tugged and yanked, but the carrot stayed put.

"It's no use," huffed Cheeks. "We'd better just run for it." Both hamsters took off running.

Too late! "Hey! What are you two doing out?" Sam set her snack on her desk and quickly scooped up a hamster in each hand. She carried them to their cage, gently put them inside, and pushed the top back down. She set a book on the roof so they wouldn't be able to escape that way again.

"Well," sighed Sir Fluffsalot, "we tried."

Miss Cookie Cheeks looked defeated. "Such a waste of a beautiful carrot," she mused.

"Whoa," Sam exclaimed. "How did this get here?" She picked up the carrot and examined it closely, but she didn't notice the little bite marks. She crossed the room, lifted the book and latch on the hamsters' cage, and plopped the carrot in. Then she finished picking up her clothes and bolted out the door.

As Cheeks and Fluffsalot gnawed their way through the delicious, healthy treat, they realized they were very lucky hamsters.

NAME: _____   DATE: _____

STEP 1: PREPARE FOR THE CHALLENGE

Problem	Challenge	Criteria	Constraints
What problem will you solve?	What will you do?	What should the solution do to be successful?	What are the limits?
The hamsters need to get from the top of the dresser to the floor quickly and safely.	Build a slide for the hamsters and give them a safe landing.	• The hamster model (three interlocking math manipulative cubes) should slide smoothly down from the starting level to the floor. • There should be a soft landing at the bottom of the slide.	• Use only the materials given. • The hamster model can't slip off the sides of the slide.

Your hamster slide will need to do two things:

1. The slide should be **steep** enough and **slippery** enough for the hamster model to slide all the way down without help.

2. Give the hamster model a place to land safely at the bottom without getting hurt.

Directions: Look over the available materials. Think about which materials you might use to accomplish each task. Sort the available materials by task in the columns below. Some materials may work in more than one category.

What materials can you use to build the slide structure?	What materials could you put on the slide that will help the hamster model slide smoothly?	How could you give the hamster model a safe landing at the bottom of the slide?

STEP 2: BRAINSTORM, PLAN, AND BUILD

1. Brainstorm design ideas for hamster slides you can build that will meet the criteria and constraints. Sketch and write at least three ideas on the back of this page. Don't forget to give the hamster model a safe landing!

2. Think about which design might perform best in testing. Draw a star by the design you will build. Why did you choose this idea?

_____

_____

_____

3. Draw a diagram of your design here. Label all of the materials.

4. Describe how your hamster slide will work.

_____

_____

_____

5. Build your hamster slide!

━━━ STEP 3: TEST, IMPROVE, AND SHARE ━━━

1. Test your hamster slide at the testing station. Did your hamster model go all the way down without stopping? If not, how could you improve your design?

> _____
>
> _____
>
> _____
>
> _____

2. Did your hamster model land safely? If not, how could you improve it?

> _____
>
> _____
>
> _____
>
> _____

3. Share your hamster slide with classmates. How can you use their ideas to make it better?

> _____
>
> _____
>
> _____

4. Keep testing and improving until your hamster slide passes the test!

STEP 4: REFLECT

1. How does your design keep the hamster model sliding all the way down?

2. How does your design help the hamster model land safely?

3. How did you improve your design?

4. What was the hardest part about this challenge?

5. What have you learned from this challenge?

PLOT SUMMARY:

Darrel wants to make cupcakes for his friend's birthday, but he has never baked before!

CUPCAKE CARRIER CHALLENGE:

| Problem
What problem will you solve? | Challenge
What will you do? | Criteria
What should the solution do to be successful? | Constraints
What are the limits? |
|---|---|---|---|
| Darrel put the cupcakes on a plate and covered them with foil. Some of the frosting stuck to the foil. | Design and build a cupcake carrier. | • The carrier should cover or enclose the cupcake completely.
• The carrier should allow you to quickly put the cupcake in and take it out.
• When carried through the testing course, the cupcake should remain unchanged. | • Use only the materials given.
• You cannot stick anything into the cupcake.
• There must not be any frosting stuck to the inside of the cupcake carrier. |

OTHER POSSIBLE PROBLEMS AND CHALLENGES:

Students can use the *Universal Challenge Pages* (pages 104–107) to create solutions to any of the problems below or problems they identify themselves.

Problem	Darrel needs to sift the flour.
Possible Challenge	• Engineer a way to sift flour using materials on hand.

Problem	Darrel drops the eggs and some break.
Possible Challenge	• Design an egg carton that protects eggs from breaking when dropped.

Problem	Darrel doesn't have a mixer, so he has to cream the butter and sugar by hand.
Possible Challenge	• Design a device to cream butter and sugar.

MATERIALS:

> **Required:** cupcakes with frosting (If you cannot use actual cupcakes, create cupcake shapes from clay or salt dough and top with shaving cream "frosting.")
>
> **Suggested:** container materials such as plastic cups and bowls, empty food containers, small cereal boxes; structural materials such as craft sticks, toothpicks, straws, cardboard; connecting materials such as tape, pipe cleaners, rubber bands

PREPARATION:

Set up a testing course for students to walk through while carrying their cupcakes. The more obstacles you add, the harder it will be for the cupcake to make it through unchanged! Some ideas for obstacles: go over a chair, go under a table, turn around in place three times, hop or jump along a masking tape line. Students can help set up the course.

LESSON PLAN:

1. Have students read the passage and discuss the problems they identified. Use these questions as prompts:

   - Have you ever baked anything? How did it go? What problems did you have? How did you solve them?
   - Did Darrel have problems in this story? How did he solve them?

2. Introduce the Cupcake Carrier Challenge by reading through the challenge pages together. Show students the available materials and review the criteria and constraints. Demonstrate (or have a student demonstrate) how they should walk the testing course.

3. Emphasize the criteria that the cupcake holders must allow the cupcakes to be put in and taken out quickly. Students can't close their carrier permanently once the cupcake is inside!

4. Give students time to prepare, brainstorm, plan, and build their cupcake carriers. Circulate to observe and answer questions as students work on their solutions. Remind them to use the challenge pages to guide them as they work through the engineering design process.

5. Have students share their solutions with the class and get feedback from peers, then revise their designs and test again.

6. When students have completed the challenge, have them explain their cupcake carrier designs to the class and demonstrate by walking the course. Then have them fill out the reflection page.

7. If time, allow students to choose their own problem and testing setup and use the *Universal Challenge Pages* (pages 104–107) to complete their challenge.

Directions: Read the passage and underline the problems the character has to face. Write and/or sketch your ideas for solutions in the margins.

BIRTHDAY BAKER

Darrel thought it would be great to make cupcakes for his friend Corbin's birthday, but he had never made cupcakes before. He had his grandma's recipe for chocolate cupcakes with chocolate frosting. He knew Corbin loved chocolate. Darrel took a deep breath and decided to give it a try.

First, he needed to measure out the ingredients. The recipe said, "Two cups of flour, sifted." What did that mean? He went to his computer and searched "how to sift flour." He learned that *sifting* means "shaking the flour through a screen." This breaks up any lumps and makes the flour lighter and easier to mix into the other ingredients. Only one problem: he didn't have a sifter. He measured out two cups of flour and stirred it a bit with a fork to break up the lumps.

The recipe called for two eggs. Darrel took a carton of eggs out of the refrigerator. As he turned to place the carton on the counter, he didn't notice his dog, Coco, behind him. He tripped over Coco, who bolted out of the kitchen. The entire carton of eggs flew out of Darrel's hand and landed on the floor. Oh, no! Thankfully, only some of the eggs broke. Darrel still had the two he needed for the cupcakes.

Once he had all the ingredients ready, Darrel moved to the instructions. He mixed together the flour, baking powder, cocoa, and salt in a bowl. Then, he read, "Cream together the butter and sugar until light and fluffy." Hmmm. Cream wasn't on the ingredient list. A quick search told him that it means to mix ingredients together quickly so little air pockets form. This makes the cupcakes fluffy. He also read that if he had an electric mixer, it would take three minutes to cream the butter and sugar. He didn't have a mixer, so he would have to cream the butter and sugar with a wooden spoon, which would take 20 minutes. By the time he was done, his arm was aching.

BIRTHDAY BAKER

He stirred the eggs into the batter, one at a time, and then the vanilla. Then he stirred in the flour mixture. Lastly, he set cupcake wrappers into a muffin tin and spooned batter into each wrapper. He put the cupcakes in the oven and set the timer. Then he breathed a sigh of relief.

Finally, the timer sounded and the cupcakes were done. As Darrel took them out of the oven, he thought they looked pretty good. He was very glad that he had bought a can of pre-made frosting. But how to get it onto the cupcakes? He searched again and found that most bakers use a piping bag to squeeze frosting on in nice patterns. He didn't have a piping bag. So he did the best he could with a spatula. He scooped out some frosting and sort of smooshed it around on each cupcake.

He put the finished cupcakes on a plate and wrapped foil over the top. When he got to Corbin's house, he wished him a happy birthday. As Corbin took the foil off of the cupcakes, Darrel could see that a lot of the frosting had stuck to the foil! Corbin didn't seem to mind. He got a butter knife and scraped some frosting off the foil and smooshed it onto a cupcake. He said it was delicious, and the smile on his face made Darrel believe it.

═══ STEP 1: PREPARE FOR THE CHALLENGE ═══

Problem — What problem will you solve?	Challenge — What will you do?	Criteria — What should the solution do to be successful?	Constraints — What are the limits?
Darrel put the cupcakes on a plate and covered them with foil. Some of the frosting stuck to the foil.	Design and build a cupcake carrier.	• The carrier should cover or enclose the cupcake completely. • The carrier should allow you to quickly put the cupcake in and take it out. • When carried through the testing course, the cupcake should remain unchanged.	• Use only the materials given. • You cannot stick anything into the cupcake. • There must not be any frosting stuck to the inside of the cupcake carrier.

Before you start designing your cupcake carrier, walk the testing course. Pay attention to each section of the course and think about what might happen to the cupcake as you are carrying it.

1. Which section of the course do you think will be the most difficult to go through without damaging the cupcake? Why?

   _____

   _____

   _____

2. What does your cupcake carrier need to do to keep your cupcake safe in this section of the course?

   _____

   _____

   _____

STEP 2: BRAINSTORM, PLAN, AND BUILD

1. Brainstorm design ideas for cupcake carriers you can build that will meet the criteria and constraints. Sketch and write at least three ideas on the back of this page.

2. Think about which design might perform best in testing. Draw a star by the design you will build. Why did you choose this idea?

_____

_____

_____

3. Draw a diagram of your design here. Label all of the materials.

4. Describe how your cupcake carrier will keep your cupcake safe throughout the testing course.

_____

_____

_____

5. Build your cupcake carrier!

STEP 3: TEST, IMPROVE, AND SHARE

1. Test your cupcake carrier. Put a cupcake in your carrier and go through the testing course holding your carrier. At the end of the course, check your cupcake. Did your cupcake carrier keep your cupcake safe? If not, what do you think went wrong?

2. How could you improve your design?

3. Share your cupcake carrier with classmates. How can you use their ideas to make it better?

4. Keep testing and improving until your cupcake carrier passes the test!

STEP 4: REFLECT

1. How does your design keep the cupcake safe?

2. How did your cupcake carrier perform the first time you tested it?

3. How did you improve your design?

4. What was the hardest part about this challenge?

5. What have you learned from this challenge?

PLOT SUMMARY:

Martina, Simon, and Lea build a not-so-spooky haunted Halloween maze for the neighborhood kids.

MOVING PROP CHALLENGE:

Problem What problem will you solve?	Challenge What will you do?	Criteria What should the solution do to be successful?	Constraints What are the limits?
Martina, Simon, and Lea want to include moving props in their haunted maze.	Design and build a prop that moves.	The prop should move in one of these ways: pop up, fly, or crawl.	• Use only the materials given. • Props cannot be permanently attached to the walls, ceiling, or floor. • Props must use kid power; no batteries or electricity.

OTHER POSSIBLE PROBLEMS AND CHALLENGES:

Students can use the *Universal Challenge Pages* (pages 104–107) to create solutions to any of the problems below or problems they identify themselves.

Problem	The kids want to build a maze in the garage.
Possible Challenge	• Build a model of a maze that isn't attached to the walls or floor.

Problem	Simon wants fog to blow through the maze.
Possible Challenge	• Design a fan to blow fog along the ground.

Problem	The kids need more fun things for the maze.
Possible Challenge	• Design and build fun props or scary items for the haunted maze.

MATERIALS:

Suggested: yarn, string, and fishing line; round items such as cardboard tubes, cans, or spools to make pulleys; long items to make levers such as rulers and yardsticks, dowels, or lumber scraps; cardboard, foam board, fabric, paint to make props

PREPARATION:

If possible, provide students with a means to record their tests on video and watch them. This will allow them to see more clearly where they need to make improvements.

LESSON PLAN:

1. Have students read the passage and discuss the problems they identified. Use these questions as prompts:

   - Have you ever been to a haunted house, a corn maze, or a fall festival? What did you do there? What did you think of it?
   - What kinds of things did the kids in this story want to make or build for their maze? What kinds of moving things did they build?

2. Introduce the Moving Prop Challenge by reading through the challenge pages together. Let students know that their prop doesn't have to be for Halloween or fall. Their prop can be for an event with any theme they like. For example, they could build a pop-up clown for a carnival, a flying reindeer for a holiday event, or a crawling caterpillar for a spring festival.

3. Talk with students about their choices in how to make their prop move: pop up, fly, and crawl. Let them know that their prop will be human powered, meaning they will have to provide a way to push or pull to make it move (it won't have batteries or use electricity). Ask them to think of things that move through pushes and pulls. Some examples: jack-in-the-boxes pop up because they are pushed up by a spring; stomp rockets pop up when they are pushed by moving air; drying clothes can "fly" when you pull on a pulley clothesline. Here are some ideas for solving this challenge:

   - Pop up: step on a long lever to pop a prop up; pull a prop up with fishing line and a pulley
   - Fly: use gravity to pull a prop down a zip line made of fishing line; use pulleys and fishing line to fly a prop across the room
   - Crawl: pull a prop along the ground with string or fishing line; put a prop on wheels and push it with a long handle

4. Show students the available materials and review the criteria and constraints. Give them time to prepare, brainstorm, plan, and build their moving props. Circulate to observe and answer questions as students work on their solutions. Remind them to use the challenge pages to guide them as they work through the engineering design process. When they are ready for testing, direct them to a space with enough room for them to test their moving prop safely.

5. Have students share their solutions with the class and get feedback from peers, then revise their designs and test again.

6. When students have completed the challenge, have them demonstrate and explain their moving props to the class. Then have them fill out the reflection page.

7. If time, allow students to choose their own problem and testing setup and use the *Universal Challenge Pages* (pages 104–107) to complete their challenge.

NAME: _____ DATE: _____

Directions: Read the passage and underline the problems the characters have to face. Write and/or sketch your ideas for solutions in the margins.

HAPPY HAUNTS

Martina, Simon, and Lea walked slowly home from school on a chilly fall Friday. Red and orange leaves drifted down around them.

Lea sighed. "Halloween isn't going to be any fun this year," she grumped.

"I know what you mean," answered Simon. "We're too old to get dressed up and go trick-or-treating, but I really want to do something."

"Come on, y'all," Martina said. "Halloween has always been my favorite holiday. I'm not going to let the fact that we are 'too old' ruin it."

"Well, what can we do?" asked Lea.

"Maybe we can help the younger kids have fun," said Martina. "Why don't we make a haunted maze for the neighborhood?!"

"Let's do it!" agreed Lea and Simon.

"Planning meeting at my house!" shouted Martina.

At Martina's, they talked about things they remembered from past haunted houses and scary mazes.

"We definitely need some ghosts," suggested Simon.

"What could we use to make them? Hmmm. I think my mom has some old sheets we could use," said Lea.

"Ghosts...check," said Martina, as she added it to the list. "Plain old sheet ghosts might be boring, though. I think we should make the ghosts fly around!" said Martina.

As they talked, they added more and more ideas to their list. The biggest project would be the maze that trick-or-treaters would walk through. Martina wanted to have spooky things pop up suddenly to make everyone jump. Lea wanted spiders that "crawl" across creepy webs. Simon thought they should get a fog machine and blow the fog through the maze. They would light up the maze with glowing eyes and plenty of jack-o'-lanterns.

HAPPY HAUNTS

"I remember that haunted hayride at the farm last year," said Lea. "There were a lot of actors in super creepy makeup and costumes, and they jumped out and scared people. Should we have people in costumes jumping out?"

"Well, this is for younger kids," said Martina, "and we don't want to scare them too much. Maybe we could ask some of our friends to dress up in Halloween costumes that aren't too scary."

"My friend Julio did some great makeup for his little brothers and sisters last Halloween," said Simon. "I'll text him and ask if he can help."

Lea laughed. "Guess we'll be dressing up for Halloween after all!"

"Hold on," said Simon. "Where exactly are we going to build this haunted maze?"

Martina ran to her dad. "Would it be okay if we build it in our garage? Pleeeease?" All three teens looked at him expectantly.

"Well," he said, "if you don't attach anything to the walls or floor, I guess it could work. And I'll tell you what: I'll supply the candy for you to pass out at the end of the maze."

The kids thanked Mr. Rosales and gave one another high fives.

All weekend, Martina, Lea, and Simon worked. As the word got out, their crew grew. By Saturday afternoon, there were over a dozen teens building and decorating the spooky maze. On Halloween night, the weather was just right—chilly with a slight breeze to rustle the leaves. Signs around the neighborhood pointed trick-or-treaters to the Happy Haunts Maze. They soon had a line of eager children waiting. Small groups of excited kids made their way past flying ghosts, pop-up scares, and crawling spiders. The air filled with screams and giggles. The three teens couldn't have been prouder.

NAME: _____   DATE: _____

STEP 1: PREPARE FOR THE CHALLENGE

Problem	Challenge	Criteria	Constraints
What problem will you solve?	What will you do?	What should the solution do to be successful?	What are the limits?
Martina, Simon, and Lea want to include moving props in their haunted maze.	Design and build a prop that moves.	The prop should move in one of these ways: pop up, fly, or crawl.	• Use only the materials given. • Props cannot be permanently attached to the walls, ceiling, or floor. • Props must use kid power; no batteries or electricity.

There are two ways to make something move: push and pull.

- When you **push** something, you move it away from you. For example, you can push a baby stroller or push a button. When you kick or throw a ball, you are pushing it. You can push down on one end of a lever to make the other end go up.

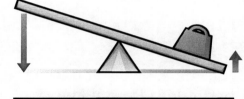

- When you **pull** something, you move it closer to you. You can pull a zipper up or down, pull on your socks, or pull a wagon. You can pull things using a pulley and string.

- Some things you can both push and pull, like a door, a drawer, or a friend on a swing. When you write, you push and pull your pencil.

Directions: Think about different ways you could use pushes and pulls to make your prop move in each way. List as many as you can think of in each category.

Pop Up	Fly	Crawl

STEP 2: BRAINSTORM, PLAN, AND BUILD

1. Brainstorm design ideas for moving props you can build that will meet the criteria and constraints. Think about how you can use pushes and pulls to make them move. Sketch and write at least three ideas on the back of this page.

2. Think about which design might perform best in testing. Draw a star by the design you will build. Why did you choose this idea?

_____

_____

_____

3. Draw a diagram of your design here. Label all of the materials.

_____

4. Describe how your moving prop will work.

_____

_____

_____

5. Build your moving prop!

▬▬▬ STEP 3: TEST, IMPROVE, AND SHARE ▬▬▬

1. Test your moving prop. Did it move in the way you planned? If not, what do you think went wrong?

_____

_____

_____

_____

2. How could you improve your design?

_____

_____

_____

_____

3. Share your moving prop with classmates. How can you use their ideas to make it better?

_____

_____

_____

4. Keep testing and improving until your moving prop works!

STEP 4: REFLECT

1. How does your prop move?

2. How did it work the first time you tested it?

3. How did you improve your design?

4. What was the hardest part about this challenge?

5. What have you learned from this challenge?

PLOT SUMMARY:

> Macie loves helping her poppa in his garden. She wants to create her own garden, but she lives in an apartment. With a little help, Macie creates a container garden on her balcony.

TOMATO PLANTER CHALLENGE:

Problem **What problem will you solve?**	Challenge **What will you do?**	Criteria **What should the solution do to be successful?**	Constraints **What are the limits?**
Macie wants to grow tomatoes in containers on her balcony.	Design and build a tomato planter.	• The planter should provide support for plants to grow tall. • The planter should allow the plants to get sunshine, air, and water. • The planter should keep squirrels from stealing tomatoes.	Use only the materials given.

OTHER POSSIBLE PROBLEMS AND CHALLENGES:

Students can use the *Universal Challenge Pages* (pages 104–107) to create solutions to any of the problems below or problems they identify themselves.

Problem	Macie needs to water her plants on the balcony.
Possible Challenges	• Design a watering can that's easy to carry or move when full. • Design a way to catch rainwater outside of the balcony and deliver it to the plants.

Problem	The apartment manager says water can't drip down onto the balcony below.
Possible Challenge	• Design a way to catch and reuse the water that drips from the plant containers.

Problem	Macie wants to see the ladybugs.
Possible Challenge	• Design a humane, temporary ladybug holder with a magnifying glass built in.

MATERIALS:

Suggested: large containers such as plant pots, plastic boxes, buckets, coffee cans, wooden boxes; open materials and fabrics such as tulle, screen, netting; clear and opaque materials such as plastic and bubble wrap, coffee filters, trash bags; structural materials such as dowels, lumber scraps, cardboard, paper cups and plates, plastic water and soda bottles, plastic cutlery, craft sticks, straws; connecting materials such as glue, tape (masking is best for this project), yarn or string, pipe cleaners; foil

Optional: tomato-plant seedlings, potting soil

LESSON PLAN:

1. Have students read the passage and discuss the problems they identified. Use these questions as prompts:

   • Have you ever been in a garden? What did you do there? What did you see, hear, and smell?
   • What did Macie want to do? What challenges did she have? How did she solve them?

2. Introduce the Tomato Planter Challenge by reading through the challenge pages together. Let students know that for this challenge they won't be testing their designs. They will design and build their tomato planter to meet three *criteria*, or requirements. Review the criteria and constraint together. Talk with students about how they might meet the criteria.

   • Students need to include something in their planter to hold up the tomato plants as they grow. Remind them that the supports must be sturdy enough to hold up the plant and also not fall apart when they get wet.
   • Students need to create a way to keep squirrels from taking the tomatoes, but they also need to be sure that sunshine and air can get to the plants and that the plants can be watered. So, for instance, they can't build a solid cardboard shield all the way around the plants because that would keep out the light and water.

   This project will require lots of brainstorming and lots of thinking about how to meet all the criteria at once. Material choices will be important!

3. Show students the available materials.

4. Give students time to prepare, brainstorm, plan, and build their tomato planters. Circulate to observe and answer questions as students work on their solutions. Remind them to use the challenge pages to guide them as they work through the engineering design process.

5. Have students share their solutions with the class and get feedback from peers, then revise and improve their designs.

6. When students have completed the challenge, you may opt to have them plant tomato seedlings in their planters. If possible, place them outside so that students can observe how well the plants grow and whether animals are able to get to the plants.

7. Have students show and explain their tomato planters to the class. Then have them fill out the reflection page.

8. If time, allow students to choose their own problem and testing setup and use the *Universal Challenge Pages* (pages 104–107) to complete their challenge.

NAME: _____   DATE: _____

Directions: Read the passage and underline the problems the characters have to face. Write and/or sketch your ideas for solutions in the margins.

▬ MACIE'S GARDEN ▬

Macie loves visiting her grandparents on the weekends. Her favorite part of her visits is working in the garden with Poppa. He grows so many delicious things, like tomatoes, peas, and peppers. In the spring, the weather warms up. She helps Poppa plant the young seedlings. She fills up the watering can and sprinkles everything carefully. All summer long, the plants need water. They grow quickly! Poppa cuts some leaves and branches off the plants. This makes room for the vegetables to grow. Together, they pull out the weeds. When the plants are ready, they harvest the vegetables. Macie loves pulling carrots and radishes out of the ground. The smell of the soil makes her happy.

Macie wants to have her own garden, but she lives in an apartment in a big building. She calls Poppa on the phone and tells him she misses him and his garden. Poppa tells her she can grow plants on her balcony. "What?" says Macie. "There isn't any soil out there!" Poppa laughs. He tells her she can grow a container garden. That means she can grow plants in boxes and pots.

Macie's mom asks the apartment manager if they can grow plants on their balcony. She says it's okay as long as water doesn't drip down on the balcony below them. Macie's mom takes her to the local co-op garden. They pick out some used pots and planter boxes. A nice lady gives her an old watering can. At the garden store, they buy a few bags of potting soil and some seedlings.

They set the containers on the balcony. Macie fills them with potting soil. She knows that vegetable plants need lots of sunlight. Her mom helps her move the containers to the sunniest spot on the balcony.

Macie plants peas and tomatoes because Poppa said they would be the easiest to grow. She fills the watering can at the kitchen sink and carries it out to

MACIE'S GARDEN

the plants. She even has to water her plants when it rains. The rain doesn't fall onto the balcony because of the roof above.

Macie cares for her plants all through the spring and into the summer. The tomato and pea plants both grow very tall. Macie needs to give them something to grow on so they don't fall over. She asks her mother to help her move the pots closer to the balcony railing. The plants grow up the railings. Lots of tomatoes and peas grow!

Macie loves to take care of her plants. She waters them and pulls out any weeds that grow in the pots. Bees and ladybugs visit the plants. Sometimes, ladybugs land on her and she watches them closely until they fly away.

One day, Macie notices that some tomatoes are missing. She watches a squirrel jump from a tree onto the balcony. It takes a tomato and scampers off. Macie doesn't mind sharing her tomatoes with the squirrels, but she hopes they don't take them all!

When the plants are ready, Macie picks tomatoes and pea pods. She helps her mom make a salad. They put some of the tomatoes and peas in the salad. They are delicious! On the weekend, Macie brings some tomatoes to her poppa. She is very proud that she grew them herself.

━━━ STEP 1: PREPARE FOR THE CHALLENGE ━━━

Problem What problem will you solve?	**Challenge** What will you do?	**Criteria** What should the solution do to be successful?	**Constraints** What are the limits?
Macie wants to grow tomatoes in containers on her balcony.	Design and build a tomato planter.	• The planter should provide support for plants to grow tall. • The planter should allow the plants to get sunshine, air, and water. • The planter should keep squirrels from stealing tomatoes.	Use only the materials given.

For this challenge, your choice of materials will be important!

1. You need to add something to your planter to hold up the tomato plants as they grow. This will help keep the plants healthy and ensure that they grow plenty of tomatoes. The materials need to be strong enough to hold up the plants without breaking, and they cannot fall apart when they get wet. You can combine materials to build a support structure.

    Which materials can you use to build supports to hold up a plant?

    _____

    _____

2. Your tomato planter must keep out squirrels, but let in sunshine, air, and water. Plants need these things to grow! Test different materials to see if they let in light by holding them up to the light or shining a flashlight through them.

    Which materials let in light?

    _____

    _____

STEP 2: BRAINSTORM, PLAN, AND BUILD

1. Brainstorm some ideas to meet each criteria for your tomato planter. Sketch and write them in the boxes below.

Supports for the plants to grow up	A way to keep out squirrels that still allows the plant to get sunshine, air, and water

2. Think about which ideas might work best. Circle the idea you will use for each criteria. Why did you choose these ideas?

_____

_____

_____

3. Combine your ideas and draw a diagram of your tomato planter design here. Label all of the materials.

4. Build your tomato planter!

STEP 3: TEST, IMPROVE, AND SHARE

1. Check to see that your tomato planter meets each criteria:

☐ Includes supports to hold up the plant

☐ Allows the plant to get sunshine, air, and water

☐ Keeps squirrels out

2. Does your tomato planter meet all the criteria? If not, how could you improve it?

_____

_____

_____

_____

_____

3. Share your tomato planter with classmates. How can you use their ideas to make it better?

_____

_____

_____

_____

_____

4. Keep redesigning until your tomato planter meets the criteria!

STEP 4: REFLECT

1. How does your design meet each criteria?

Includes supports to hold up the plant: _____

Allows the plant to get sunshine, air, and water: _____

_____

Keeps squirrels out: _____

2. How did you improve your design?

_____

_____

_____

_____

3. What was the hardest part about this challenge?

_____

_____

_____

4. What have you learned from this challenge?

_____

_____

_____

PLOT SUMMARY:

Princess Petra goes on a quest for treasure, aided by her new dress with magic pockets.

RIVER CROSSING CHALLENGE:

Problem What problem will you solve?	Challenge What will you do?	Criteria What should the solution do to be successful?	Constraints What are the limits?
Princess Petra needs to get across the river safely.	Engineer a way to move Petra across the river safely.	The princess model should get from one side of the river to the other safely.	• Use only the materials given. • The river crossing device must not attach to the ground. It must be freestanding. • Don't break the princess model!

OTHER POSSIBLE PROBLEMS AND CHALLENGES:

Students can use the *Universal Challenge Pages* (pages 104–107) to create solutions to any of the problems below or problems they identify themselves.

Problem	Princess Petra needs to get up to the cliff fortress window safely.
Possible Challenge	• Engineer something to move Petra safely up to the window.

Problem	Princess Petra needs to play music to put the dragon to sleep.
Possible Challenge	• Make a string, wind, or percussion instrument that you can play.

Problem	Princess Petra needs a way to carry the heavy treasure box.
Possible Challenges	• Build a carrier with wheels to help her move the treasure. • Engineer another way to move the treasure.

Problem	Princess Petra needs to get down from the fortress safely.
Possible Challenge	• Engineer something to move Petra safely from the fortress down to the ground.

MATERIALS:

Required: small dolls or action figures of a similar size and weight, one per team; large pan or tub for "river"; water; rulers; paper towels

Suggested: structural items such as wooden skewers, straws, craft sticks, cardstock or index cards, dry spaghetti, plastic cutlery; materials to carry or control, such as paper and plastic cups, egg cartons, plastic water bottles; string-like materials such as fishing line, string, and yarn; connectors such as paper clips, binder clips, rubber bands, tape

PREPARATION:

Set up a table or desk for testing. Create a "river" for the "princess" to cross by filling a large pan or tub with an inch or two of water. The wider the river, the more difficult this challenge will be. You may want to set up several identical rivers for testing so multiple teams can test at the same time. Each team will need a small doll or action figure "princess" for testing—any small characters will do, as long as they are of similar size and weight. Provide paper towels for spills.

LESSON PLAN:

1. Have students read the passage and discuss the problems they identified. Use these questions as prompts:

    - What problems did Princess Petra have in getting to the treasure? What problems did she encounter in bringing the treasure home with her?
    - How did Princess Petra solve her problems? Are her solutions realistic?
    - Can you think of real-world solutions to Petra's problems?

2. Introduce the River Crossing Challenge by reading through the challenge pages together. Show students the available materials and review the criteria and constraints. Show students the "river" they will need to transport their princess safely across. They can engineer any solution to the problem that gets their princess to the other side safely. Some ideas: a bridge, a raft or boat, a zip line, an aerial cable car.

3. Give students time to prepare, brainstorm, plan, and build their river crossing prototypes. Circulate to observe and answer questions as students work on their solutions. Remind them to use the challenge pages to guide them as they work through the engineering design process. When they are ready for testing, observe to ensure fair and equal testing conditions for each student or team.

4. Have students share their solutions with the class and get feedback from peers, then revise their designs and test again.

5. When students have completed the challenge, have them demonstrate and explain their river crossing devices to the class. Then have them fill out the reflection page.

6. If time, allow students to choose their own problem and testing setup and use the *Universal Challenge Pages* (pages 104–107) to complete their challenge.

Directions: Read the passage and underline the problems the character has to face. Write and/or sketch your ideas for solutions in the margins.

◼ MAGIC POCKETS ◼

Princess Petra had always wanted pockets. All of her dresses, skirts, and ball gowns were beautiful. They sparkled in bright colors and looked amazing when she twirled. But none of them had pockets. She made a wish out loud for a dress with pockets, and *ZING!* There in her closet was a new dress. It wasn't the most beautiful dress in the world, and it didn't sparkle. When Petra put the dress on, it was surprisingly comfortable. She plunged her hands into the deep pockets of the dress and smiled.

As a princess, Petra was always going on quests. It was part of the job. Today's quest was to the cliff fortress of Acantilado to bring home the stolen Treasure of Oa.

On her journey, Petra came to the Daraja River. It was very wide and flowed very quickly. How would she get across? Petra put her hands into her pockets to think. She felt something in her right-hand pocket. She pulled out a small box with a red button on top labeled "Push Me." Petra shrugged, thought, "Why not?" and pushed the button. She stumbled backwards as a full-sized bridge unfolded from the box and spanned the river. Petra ran across the bridge and pushed the button when she was safely on the other side. The bridge folded itself back into the little box, and Petra put the box back in her pocket. These pockets were going to be handy!

As she approached the Cliffs of Doom, she could see the windows of the fortress of Acantilado high above her. Petra wished she had a magic carpet so she could just fly up there. She put her hand in her pocket and felt something soft. She pulled...and pulled and pulled. Out came a carpet! She unrolled it and watched in awe as it floated above the ground. She sat carefully on the carpet. It was tricky keeping her balance as the carpet flew her up to a window.

MAGIC POCKETS

Petra climbed in through the window and found herself in a long hallway. She tiptoed quietly from door to door, carefully peeking into each one.

She found the kitchen, a bathroom, and several bedrooms, but no treasure room. Finally, at the very end of the hallway, she came upon a huge room filled with glittering jewels and shining gold. The only problem was the huge dragon guarding the treasure.

Petra put her hand in her pocket and pulled out a harp. Petra didn't know how to play the harp, but that didn't seem to matter. As she plucked the strings, out flowed a beautiful melody. Slowly, the dragon's eyelids lowered, until it was sound asleep and snoring. Petra tiptoed past into the treasure room. She searched through the jewels and gold until she found the huge box containing the Treasure of Oa. It was heavy!

Petra put her hand into her pocket once again and pulled out a wheelbarrow. She pushed the treasure box into the wheelbarrow. It was surprisingly easy to push the wheelbarrow down the hall to the window where she had come in. But how would she get the treasure back down to the ground?

Magic pockets to the rescue once again! This time, she pulled out a magic rope. She tied the rope around the treasure box and around her waist. She climbed onto the treasure box, and the magic rope lowered them safely to the ground.

One last time, Petra plunged her hands into her pockets. This time, she pulled out a carriage, complete with four horses. As she rode home to her palace with the treasure, she wondered what else she would find in her magic pockets. She knew this was her new favorite dress!

STEP 1: PREPARE FOR THE CHALLENGE

Problem What problem will you solve?	**Challenge** What will you do?	**Criteria** What should the solution do to be successful?	**Constraints** What are the limits?
Princess Petra needs to get across the river safely.	Engineer a way to move Petra across the river safely.	The princess model should get from one side of the river to the other safely.	• Use only the materials given. • The river crossing device must not attach to the ground. It must be freestanding. • Don't break the princess model!

Directions: Carefully examine the "river" that the princess will need to cross. Draw a diagram of it here. Include measurements! Use this diagram as you are planning your solution.

━━━ STEP 2: BRAINSTORM, PLAN, AND BUILD ━━━

1. Brainstorm design ideas to get the princess safely from one side of the river to the other. Your plans must meet the criteria and constraints. Don't forget to look at the diagram you made of the river. Sketch and write at least three ideas on the back of this page.

2. Think about which design might perform best in testing. Draw a star by the design you will build. Why did you choose this idea?

_____

_____

_____

3. Draw a diagram of your design here. Label all of the materials.

4. Describe how your idea will get the princess safely across the river.

_____

_____

_____

5. Build your river crossing device!

STEP 3: TEST, IMPROVE, AND SHARE

1. Test your river crossing device at the testing station. Did your princess get across the river safely? If not, where or how did it fail?

_____

_____

_____

_____

2. How could you improve your design?

_____

_____

_____

_____

3. Share your river crossing device with classmates. How can you use their ideas to make it better?

_____

_____

_____

4. Keep testing and improving until your river crossing device passes the test!

STEP 4: REFLECT

1. How does your device move the princess across the river?

2. How did your device work the first time you tested it?

3. How did you improve your device?

4. What was the hardest part about this challenge?

5. What have you learned from this challenge?

PLOT SUMMARY:

Potato the porcupine was rescued as a baby. She now lives in a zoo. Her keepers work hard to meet her needs and keep her happy.

ZOO HABITAT CHALLENGE:

Problem What problem will you solve?	**Challenge** What will you do?	**Criteria** What should the solution do to be successful?	**Constraints** What are the limits?
Potato the porcupine needs a new habitat at the zoo.	Design and build a model zoo habitat for Potato.	• The habitat should keep Potato safe and visible. • The habitat should include a warm den for sleeping, a climbing structure, fresh water, and a place for keepers to keep tools so Potato won't chew on them.	Use only the materials given.

OTHER POSSIBLE PROBLEMS AND CHALLENGES:

Students can use the *Universal Challenge Pages* (pages 104–107) to create solutions to any of the problems below or problems they identify themselves.

Problem	Potato likes to be held.
Possible Challenge	• Design a way for keepers to hold Potato without getting quilled.

Problem	Keepers need Potato to go into her crate.
Possible Challenge	• Design something to help the keepers safely get Potato to go into her crate.

Problem	Keepers want Potato to get exercise.
Possible Challenge	• Design enrichment toys for a porcupine.

MATERIALS:

Suggested: structural materials such as craft sticks, straws, unsharpened pencils, cardboard sheets and boxes, cardstock and index cards, paper and plastic cups and plates, empty food containers, paper towel and toilet paper rolls; natural materials such as sticks, leaves, and rocks; connecting materials such as glue, string, rubber bands, pipe cleaners, tape; paint

PREPARATION:

While students will not be testing their designs in this project, you will need a space for them to display their models so that everyone can examine them and give feedback.

LESSON PLAN:

1. Have students read the passage and discuss the problems they identified. Use these questions as prompts:

   • Have you ever seen a porcupine? What other animals have you seen?
   • Do you have a pet? How do you care for it?
   • What challenges do the zookeepers have in taking care of Potato? Did they solve any of them? How?

2. Introduce the Zoo Habitat Challenge by reading through the challenge pages together. Explain to students that they will be creating a model of a porcupine zoo habitat. Let students know that for this challenge they won't be testing their designs. They will design and build their model habitat to meet criteria, or requirements.

3. Ask students to use what they learned about porcupines in the reading to design a zoo habitat. Remind them that porcupines are great climbers and that they like to chew on wood and rubber. Because this is a model, they can use whatever materials they have access to, but they should label them to show what would be used in a full-size enclosure. For example, they can use craft sticks to build part of the enclosure, even though porcupines chew on wood, as long as they label them something like "metal poles" and paint them so they don't look like wood.

4. Show students the available materials and review the criteria and constraint. Give them time to think about the materials and complete the tasks for Step 1 (page 68). This will give them examples of floor plans to help them draw their own.

5. Give students time to prepare, brainstorm, plan, and build their zoo habitats. Circulate to observe and answer questions as students work on their solutions. Remind them to use the challenge pages to guide them as they work through the engineering design process.

6. Have students evaluate their models by checking them against the criteria, and then share their solutions with the class and get feedback from peers. Then they should revise and improve their designs.

7. When students have completed the challenge, have them show and explain their model zoo habitats to the class. Then have them fill out the reflection page.

8. If time, allow students to choose their own problem and testing setup and use the *Universal Challenge Pages* (pages 104–107) to complete their challenge.

Directions: Read the passage and underline the problems the characters have to face. Write and/or sketch your ideas for solutions in the margins.

POTATO THE PORCUPINE

Potato the porcupine was found by the side of a road when she was a little baby porcupette. Her mother had been hit by a car. Potato was too young to take care of herself in the wild. Rescuers took her in and raised her. They named her Potato because she was about the size of a baked potato. She can't go back to the wild because she hasn't learned how to find food and avoid predators. Now, Potato lives in a small zoo where people can see her and learn about porcupines.

Potato has over 30,000 quills covering most of her body. Quills are hard, hollow hairs with barbed points on the end. Those hollow quills float, which makes porcupines good swimmers! No, porcupines cannot shoot their quills. When a porcupine feels threatened, it can slap at a predator with its tail. If the predator gets too close, it will get a face full of quills. The quills are not easy to remove. The barbed tip is like a tiny fishhook. It keeps the quill buried in the skin. As a defense mechanism, a porcupine's quills are very effective! Who would want a bite of that? The only place a porcupine is vulnerable it its soft, quill-less belly.

Potato's quills pose a challenge for the zookeepers. Quills grow like fur or hair, in one direction. You can pet a porcupine from front to back. But if you try to push a porcupine forward from behind, you'll get a handful of quills! This makes it a challenge to get Potato into her crate. Potato loves to be held, but keepers must wear thick, leather gloves when they carry her.

Porcupines are *arboreal*. This means they spend most of their time in trees. They have long, strong claws for climbing. Keepers set up a structure of thick branches in Potato's habitat. This gives her places to climb and explore. Potato also enjoys hanging upside down. It's like a playground climbing structure for porcupines!

POTATO THE PORCUPINE

When the weather is cold, keepers put straw in a hollow log for Potato to crawl into. The problem is that she chews on the log!

Porcupines are *herbivores*, or plant eaters. In the wild, they eat leaves, pine needles, nuts, and fruit. In the zoo, Potato gets sweet potatoes, carrots, and lettuce. She also gets special pellets made for large rodents like porcupines and beavers. Like all rodents, a porcupine's front teeth are constantly growing. Chewing and gnawing on bark and wood keeps their teeth from growing too long. Keepers make sure Potato has plenty of browse to chew on. *Browse* is branches cut from trees and bushes. And keepers are careful not to leave their rakes and gloves in Potato's habitat. She will chew on anything made of wood or rubber!

Porcupines don't see very well, but they have a good sense of smell. To make sure she gets her exercise, keepers hide some of Potato's food around her habitat. She uses her nose to find yummy treats high up in the branches. She uses her long, strong claws to turn over logs and rocks to get food hidden underneath. Keepers also make sure Potato always has fresh water to drink.

Lately, Potato's keepers have noticed that she has been chewing on the wooden beams holding up her enclosure. They are worried that she could chew all the way through them. They don't want the whole thing to fall down! They are now making plans for a new habitat for Potato. She will have a long, happy life at the zoo.

STEP 1: PREPARE FOR THE CHALLENGE

Problem What problem will you solve?	Challenge What will you do?	Criteria What should the solution do to be successful?	Constraints What are the limits?
Potato the porcupine needs a new habitat at the zoo.	Design and build a model zoo habitat for Potato.	• The habitat should keep Potato safe and visible. • The habitat should include a warm den for sleeping, a climbing structure, fresh water, and a place for keepers to keep tools so Potato won't chew on them.	Use only the materials given.

People who design zoo habitats must draw a floor plan of their design. A *floor plan* is a view as if you are looking down from above. Look at the floor plan of a bear zoo habitat and answer the questions below.

1. Highlight along the area where visitors can look in and see the bears.

2. Draw an **X** on the area where the keepers can store their tools.

3. Circle the gate where the bears can go from their sleeping area to the main enclosure.

4. What five things did the designers put in the bears' habitat to keep them busy?

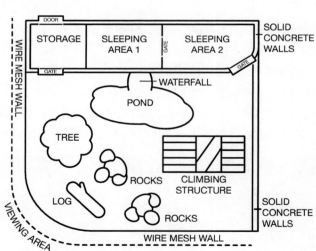

_____

_____

STEP 2: BRAINSTORM, PLAN, AND BUILD

1. Brainstorm design ideas to meet the criteria and constraint. Sketch and write at least three ideas on the back of this page. Think about the following:

    • What materials can you use for the enclosure that will keep Potato safe inside and will allow visitors to see her?

    • How big should the habitat be to include everything Potato needs? What shape will it be?

2. Think about which design ideas might work best. Circle the idea you will use. Why did you choose this idea?

    _____

    _____

    _____

3. Draw a floor plan of your zoo habitat design here. Label all of the materials you will use to build the model. In parentheses next to these labels, write what materials would be used in a real habitat.

4. Build your model zoo habitat!

STEP 3: TEST, IMPROVE, AND SHARE

1. Check to see that your zoo habitat meets each criteria:

☐ The enclosure will keep Potato safe inside.

☐ Visitors can see Potato in her enclosure.

☐ Potato has a warm place to sleep.

☐ Potato has a structure to climb.

☐ Potato has access to fresh water.

☐ Keepers have a place to store tools where Potato can't chew them.

2. Does your zoo habitat design meet all the criteria? If not, how could you improve it?

_____

_____

_____

_____

3. Share your zoo habitat with classmates. How can you use their ideas to make it better?

_____

_____

_____

_____

4. Keep redesigning until your zoo habitat meets the criteria!

STEP 4: REFLECT

1. How does your design meet each criteria?

The enclosure will keep Potato safe inside: _____

Visitors can see Potato in her enclosure: _____

Potato has a warm place to sleep: _____

Potato has a structure to climb: _____

Potato has access to fresh water: _____

Keepers have a place to store tools where Potato can't chew them:

_____

2. How did you improve your design?

_____

_____

_____

3. What was the hardest part about this challenge?

_____

_____

_____

4. What have you learned from this challenge?

_____

_____

PLOT SUMMARY:

This is the traditional tale of "Jack and the Beanstalk," told from the giant's point of view.

BEANSTALK TOWER CHALLENGE:

Problem What problem will you solve?	**Challenge** What will you do?	**Criteria** What should the solution do to be successful?	**Constraints** What are the limits?
The giant needs to get back up to his home.	Build a "beanstalk" tower that can hold weight at the top.	• The tower should be at least one foot tall. • The tower should hold a weight at the top. • A successful tower should stand for at least as long as it takes to measure it and write down its height.	• Use only the materials given. • The tower cannot be attached to the ground or anything else. It must be freestanding.

OTHER POSSIBLE PROBLEMS AND CHALLENGES:

Students can use the *Universal Challenge Pages* (pages 104–107) to create solutions to any of the problems below or problems they identify themselves.

Problem	The giant needs a way to keep track of his coins so he doesn't have to count them every day.
Possible Challenge	• Engineer a money-storage device that counts coins or sorts them in a way that makes the number of coins easy to see.

Problem	The giant needs to safeguard his harp and golden goose.
Possible Challenges	• Engineer an alarm system. • Design a trap to catch Jack. • Build something to safeguard the giant's possessions.

Problem	The giant wants to catch Jack to talk to him.
Possible Challenge	• Engineer a device the giant can use to safely catch Jack.

MATERIALS:

Required: near-identical spherical objects (one per team) to use as model "giants," such as tennis balls, apples, or hard-boiled eggs (the heavier the objects, the more difficult this challenge will be); yardsticks or tape measures

Suggested: structural materials such as craft sticks, straws, paper or index cards, paper or plastic cups; connecting materials such as tape, glue, string, pipe cleaners, play clay

PREPARATION:

The difficulty of this challenge will depend on the materials available and will result in different-sized towers. Students may build towers much taller than you expect, so consider having them build on the ground so they can reach the top of their tower without having to climb on furniture.

LESSON PLAN:

1. Have students read the passage and discuss the problems they identified. Use these questions as prompts:

   - Do you recognize this story? What versions have you heard before?
   - What problems did the giant have? Did he solve any of them? How?
   - Can you think of solutions to the giant's problems?

2. Introduce the Beanstalk Tower Challenge by reading through the challenge pages together. Show students the available materials and review the criteria and constraints. Show students the model "giant" they will need to support at the top of their tower.

3. Give students time to prepare, brainstorm, plan, and build their towers. Circulate to observe and answer questions as students work on their solutions. Remind them to use the challenge pages to guide them as they work through the engineering design process. When they are ready for testing, observe and, if needed, help students measure their towers. They will need to be careful not to knock them down!

4. Have students share their solutions with the class and get feedback from peers, then revise their designs and test again.

5. When students have completed the challenge, have them demonstrate and explain their beanstalk towers to the class. Then have them fill out the reflection page.

6. If time, allow students to choose their own problem and testing setup and use the *Universal Challenge Pages* (pages 104–107) to complete their challenge.

Directions: Read the passage and underline the problems the characters have to face. Write and/or sketch your ideas for solutions in the margins.

FEE FI FO FUM

It all started with some missing coins. Every afternoon, I sit in my treasure room and count my gold coins. One day, I came up one coin short. At first, I thought I miscounted, so I counted again. I wondered if I was getting forgetful. Maybe I dropped it without noticing. But the next day, another coin went missing. Something strange was going on.

When I get up in the morning, I always look forward to breakfast. I make a big omelet with golden eggs from my special goose. The gold really adds to the flavor! One morning, I went to get an egg from the nest, but the goose wasn't there. I figured she had flown south for the winter. Since the loss of my goose, I only eat toast for breakfast.

The worst thing that happened was that my magic harp disappeared. This was a problem! Every night, my harp sings a beautiful melody to put me to sleep. Without its soothing song, I haven't been able to sleep for days.

This morning, as I was sleepily chewing my toast, I smelled an awful smell. I sniffed the air. I looked around, but I didn't see anything out of the ordinary. Still, that bad odor seemed to be everywhere.

As I took a sip of my coffee, out of the corner of my eye, I saw something move on the kitchen counter. I quietly tiptoed over and peeked behind the toaster. I was shocked! I found a little man, and boy was he smelly. He definitely hadn't had a shower in a while.

I exclaimed:

Fee fi fo fum,
Where on Earth did you come from?
Are you the one who stole my stuff?
Now I found you, sure enough!

FEE FI FO FUM

The miniature man took off. Across the kitchen counter and around the sink he ran. He shimmied down the dishtowel and jumped to the floor. By the time I had recovered my wits, he was out the front door.

I chased him across the front garden and out the gate. He sure was fast for a teeny guy! I guess he thought I wanted to hurt him, but I only wanted to ask him to bring back my stuff.

Ahead, I saw a strange-looking plant. The mini man scrambled onto it and disappeared. When I got closer, I could see that this was just the tip of an incredibly tall beanstalk. Because I was so bewildered by these strange circumstances, I made a poor decision. I decided to climb down the beanstalk after the little man. That was not a good idea.

I am a fairly big guy, and the beanstalk was just not strong enough to hold me. It started to sway back and forth as I held on for dear life. I could hear it creaking and cracking. Then, whoa! The whole thing toppled over and down I fell. The last thing I remember is the little man yelling, "Look out!"

So now I'm stuck here in this land full of tiny people. My head hurts and I skinned my knee. Jack apologized for stealing my things, and he and his mother are doing their best to make me feel welcome. But the food here is just so small; I'm hungry all the time. I have to sleep on the ground because I don't fit in any of the beds. At least I have my magic harp to sing me to sleep.

NAME: _____   DATE: _____

STEP 1: PREPARE FOR THE CHALLENGE

Problem What problem will you solve?	Challenge What will you do?	Criteria What should the solution do to be successful?	Constraints What are the limits?
The giant needs to get back up to his home.	Build a "beanstalk" tower that can hold weight at the top.	• The tower should be at least one foot tall. • The tower should hold a weight at the top. • A successful tower should stand for at least as long as it takes to measure it and write down its height.	• Use only the materials given. • The tower cannot be attached to the ground or anything else. It must be freestanding.

A **tower** is a structure that is taller than it is wide. Here are some real-world examples of towers.

What do the examples have in common? What do you see that you might be able to use in your tower design?

_____

_____

_____

STEP 2: BRAINSTORM, PLAN, AND BUILD

1. Brainstorm design ideas for towers you can build that will meet the criteria and constraints. Remember, your tower must hold the "giant" at the top. Sketch and write at least three ideas on the back of this page.

2. Think about which design might perform best in testing. Draw a star by the design you will build. Why did you choose this idea?

_____

_____

_____

3. Draw a diagram of your design here. Label all of the materials.

4. Describe how your tower will hold up the weight of the "giant."

_____

_____

_____

_____

_____

_____

_____

_____

_____

_____

5. Build your beanstalk tower!

═══ STEP 3: TEST, IMPROVE, AND SHARE ═══

1. Place the "giant" at the top of your tower. Did it stay up? If not, how could you improve your design so it stays up with the "giant" in place?

_____

_____

_____

_____

2. Once your tower stays up with the "giant" in place, measure the height of your tower. How could you improve your design to make it taller?

_____

_____

_____

_____

3. Share your tower with classmates. How can you use their ideas to make it better?

_____

_____

_____

_____

4. Keep testing and improving until your tower is as tall as it can be with the "giant" on top!

STEP 4: REFLECT

1. How does your tower hold up the weight of the "giant"?

_____

_____

_____

_____

2. How did you improve your design?

_____

_____

_____

_____

3. What was the hardest part about this challenge?

_____

_____

_____

4. What have you learned from this challenge?

_____

_____

_____

PLOT SUMMARY:

Kory is bored. When his mom brings him a box full of all kinds of paper, he lets his imagination loose.

PAPER CHAIN CHALLENGE:

Problem What problem will you solve?	Challenge What will you do?	Criteria What should the solution do to be successful?	Constraints What are the limits?
Kory's paper chain isn't strong enough to hold his books.	Build a paper chain that holds as much weight as possible.	• The chain should hold at least the empty bucket without breaking. • The chain should be at least two feet long.	Use only paper and tape.

OTHER POSSIBLE PROBLEMS AND CHALLENGES:

Students can use the *Universal Challenge Pages* (pages 104–107) to create solutions to any of the problems below or problems they identify themselves.

Problem	Kory wants his boat to hold weight without sinking.
Possible Challenge	• Engineer a paper boat to hold weights.

Problem	Kory's paper airplanes don't fly very well.
Possible Challenge	• Design and test paper airplanes.

Problem	Kory's marble roller coaster doesn't work at first.
Possible Challenge	• Design a marble roller coaster.

MATERIALS:

Required: different kinds of paper—construction paper, newspaper, or used writing/copy paper; masking tape and scissors; five-gallon bucket with a sturdy, well-attached handle; large S-hooks, carabiners, or zip ties; books to use as weights for testing

PREPARATION:

You will need an identical bucket for each team for testing. Five-gallon buckets work well, but it could be any big container with a sturdy handle that isn't easy to pull off. The books should be of an identical or at least similar size and weight to keep testing fair. Class sets of novels or composition books work well. You could use water instead of books if you can test outdoors.

LESSON PLAN:

1. Have students read the passage and discuss the problems they identified. Use these questions as prompts:

   • Have you ever been bored? Where were you? What did you do about it?
   • Did Kory have any problems while he was building? How did he solve them?

2. Introduce the Paper Chain Challenge by reading through the challenge pages together. Show students the available materials and review the criteria and constraint. Explain that they will attach their paper chain to the handle of the bucket with an S-hook, carabiner, or zip tie. Then, holding on to only their paper chain, they should lift the bucket just high enough that it is not touching the ground. If the chain can hold the empty bucket, they can add books one at a time.

3. Give students time to prepare, brainstorm, plan, and build their paper chains. Circulate to observe and answer questions as students work on their solutions. Remind them to use the challenge pages to guide them as they work through the engineering design process. When they are ready for testing, observe to ensure fair and equal testing conditions for each student or team.

4. Have students share their solutions with the class and get feedback from peers, then revise their designs and test again.

5. When students have completed the challenge, have them demonstrate and explain their paper chain to the class. If desired, you can have a competition to see which paper chain holds the most weight.

6. Have students fill out the reflection page.

7. If time, allow students to choose their own problem and testing setup and use the *Universal Challenge Pages* (pages 104–107) to complete their challenge.

Directions: Read the passage and underline the problems the character has to face. Write and/or sketch your ideas for solutions in the margins.

BORED

Kory was bored. Really bored. The kind of bored that comes when you're stuck at home on a rainy afternoon. He laid on his bed and stared at the raindrops rolling down the window.

His mom walked into his room carrying a box. She plopped it down on the floor.

"What's that?" asked Kory.

"Something for you to do." His mom smiled.

Kory peered into the box. He saw lots of different kinds of paper: newspaper, construction paper, copy paper, index cards, paper bags, and some paper towel and toilet paper rolls. There were also a pair of scissors, a roll of masking tape, and a roll of clear tape.

"What can you make with that?" asked his mom. She left and closed the door behind her.

Kory began taking the paper out of the box. He sorted it into piles. As he looked over the materials, he thought about what he could make. He grabbed one of the sheets of plain copy paper and started to sketch.

He started by drawing the outline of a paper airplane. He added some windows and a little pilot. Then he drew a paper boat with a tiny ship's wheel helmed by a tiny captain. He designed a flag for his boat and a figurehead that looked like his favorite cartoon character.

Kory's imagination really began to fly! He sketched a theme park full of rides: a roller coaster, a drop tower, a Ferris wheel, and a spinning ride. A giant maze formed on his paper, with dead ends, blind alleys, tunnels, and a tower in the center. He imagined the huge tower reaching to the sky so he could look out over the whole maze. He designed a library with marble columns and a staircase in front. Inside, he sketched rows of books

BORED

on two levels with a moveable ladder to reach all the books.

Kory's sketching hand was getting tired, so he started building. He cut strips of construction paper and made a long paper chain. He hung it over his bed. Next, he made a basket out of a paper bag. He tried to hang the basket from the paper chain, but the chain wasn't strong enough. He fixed the chain and hung it back up. He set the basket on his desk to hold books.

Kory folded some paper airplanes and flew them across the room. They didn't fly all that well, but it was fun to try! He made a paper boat and took it to the bathroom. He put some water in the sink and set sail. To test how buoyant his boat was, he filled it with things. It sailed beautifully holding his toothbrush and a package of dental floss. It stayed afloat until he added a bar of soap. *Glub, glub*, down it sank. He made a new version of the boat, and this time, it held all three!

Kory looked through his sketches again. He really liked the theme park, so he started building a marble roller coaster. He folded index cards to make sections of the track and taped it all together. He used the paper towel and toilet paper rolls to hold up the track at different levels. The marble didn't roll smoothly through the whole track at first. He had to test it and make changes many times. Finally, he got the marble to roll all the way down the roller coaster. He folded some construction paper into a little cup for the marble to fall into at the end.

Kory kept building all afternoon. When his mom came to call him for dinner, she gasped at what she saw. His whole room was filled with amazing paper structures. "Well," she said, "I guess you're not bored anymore!"

NAME: _____   **DATE:** _____

═══ STEP 1: PREPARE FOR THE CHALLENGE ═══

Problem What problem will you solve?	**Challenge** What will you do?	**Criteria** What should the solution do to be successful?	**Constraints** What are the limits?
Kory's paper chain isn't strong enough to hold his books.	Build a paper chain that holds as much weight as possible.	• The chain should hold at least the empty bucket without breaking. • The chain should be at least two feet long.	Use only paper and tape.

Directions: Make and test a simple paper chain.

1. Cut a sheet of paper into five strips. The strips should be about the same width and length.
2. Tape the ends of one strip together to make a loop.
3. Put another strip of paper through the first link and tape it into a loop.
4. Repeat until you have five links in your paper chain.
5. Test the strength of your paper chain by pulling each end in opposite directions until it breaks. Pay close attention to where the chain **fails**, or comes apart.

Directions: Answer the questions below.

1. What part or parts of the chain are the weakest? How could you strengthen those parts?

   _____

   _____

2. How could you change the paper to make it stronger? How could you fold, twist, or roll it?

   _____

   _____

STEP 2: BRAINSTORM, PLAN, AND BUILD

1. Brainstorm design ideas for paper chains you can build that will meet the criteria and constraint. Sketch and write at least three ideas on the back of this page.

2. Think about which design might perform best in testing. Draw a star by the design you will build. Why did you choose this idea?

_____

_____

_____

3. Draw a diagram of your design here.

4. Why do you think this design will hold the most weight?

_____

_____

_____

5. Build your paper chain!

STEP 3: TEST, IMPROVE, AND SHARE

1. Measure the length of your chain to be sure it is at least two feet long. If not, add more links to make it longer.

2. Test your paper chain by hanging a bucket from it. Did your paper chain hold the empty bucket? If so, add books, one at a time, until the chain breaks. Describe what happens.

_____

_____

_____

3. How could you improve your chain so that it holds more weight? Build a new version and test it again. Make sure your new version is long enough to meet the criteria!

_____

_____

_____

4. Share your paper chain with classmates. How can you use their ideas to make it better?

_____

_____

_____

5. Keep testing and improving your paper chain!

STEP 4: REFLECT

1. How did you design the first version of your paper chain?

_____

_____

_____

_____

2. How did you improve the design?

_____

_____

_____

3. What was the hardest part about this challenge?

_____

_____

_____

4. What have you learned from this challenge?

_____

_____

_____

PLOT SUMMARY:

Alanna and Gus work hard to clean up their local park so they can enjoy their picnic.

POLLUTION BARRIER CHALLENGE:

Problem What problem will you solve?	Challenge What will you do?	Criteria What should the solution do to be successful?	Constraints What are the limits?
Pollution from the street and parking lot is washing into the pond when it rains.	Engineer a way to keep pollution from getting into the pond.	The pollution barrier should keep two spoonfuls of oily water out of the pond area, so the paper towel "pond" should stay completely dry.	• Use only the materials given. • The pollution barrier cannot be attached to the container.

OTHER POSSIBLE PROBLEMS AND CHALLENGES:

Students can use the *Universal Challenge Pages* (pages 104–107) to create solutions to any of the problems below or problems they identify themselves.

Problem	The kids want to pick up litter safely.
Possible Challenges	• Design a litter-picker-upper to safely pick up litter on the ground. • Design a litter-picker-upper to safely pick up litter in the water.

Problem	The kids are worried about the pollution in the pond hurting the duck.
Possible Challenge	• Engineer a way to clean oil from water.

Problem	The kids want to encourage others to keep the park clean.
Possible Challenge	• Design a trash can that separates recyclables and tells others how to keep the park clean.

MATERIALS:

Required: identical large, shallow containers (e.g., plastic washtub, large aluminum tray) and spoons, one per team; 1/4 cups; vegetable oil, cocoa powder, and water to make "oil"; small toys of similar size for duck models; paper towels

Suggested: absorbent materials such as cotton balls, fabric, sponges (cut into smaller pieces); nonabsorbent materials such as aluminum foil, plastic wrap, wax paper, bubble wrap; structural materials such as straws, craft sticks, toothpicks, cardboard tubes; connectors such as rubber bands, yarn or string, tape

PREPARATION:

Prepare water polluted with "oil" by mixing 1/4 cup of vegetable oil and a few teaspoons of cocoa powder into a gallon of water. Set cups with small amounts of "polluted" water and empty large, shallow containers out for testing. Provide paper towels for spills.

LESSON PLAN:

1. Have students read the passage and discuss the problems they identified. Use these questions as prompts:

   • When was the last time you went to a park? Did you see any pollution?
   • How did Alanna and Gus clean up the park?
   • Do you think it's important to clean up pollution? Why or why not?

2. Introduce the Pollution Barrier Challenge by reading through the challenge pages together. Show students the available materials and review the criteria and constraints. Explain to students that they will be creating a model pond and pollution barrier. To test their models, students will place their duck (small toy) on a paper towel (representing the pond) at one end of a testing container and place their pollution barrier model across the middle of the container to protect the pond. For testing, they will pour two spoonfuls of "polluted" water in the area on the other side of their pollution barrier model. Assure them that the water is not polluted with real motor oil and it is safe for them to handle.

3. For Step 1 of the challenge (page 92), students will need access to the materials, along with a cup of water. These tests will require spilling water, so either provide shallow containers for students to do their tests in or have students test their materials outside.

4. Give students time to prepare, brainstorm, plan, and build their pollution barriers. Circulate to observe and answer questions as students work on their solutions. Remind them to use the challenge pages to guide them as they work through the engineering design process.

5. When students are ready to test their pollution barriers, direct them to the testing area. They will know their barrier worked if their paper towel stays dry. Have students share their solutions with the class and get feedback from peers, then revise their designs and test again.

6. When students have completed the challenge, have them demonstrate and explain their pollution barriers to the class. Then have them fill out the reflection page.

7. If time, allow students to choose their own problem and testing setup and use the *Universal Challenge Pages* (pages 104–107) to complete their challenge.

Directions: Read the passage and underline the problems the characters have to face. Write and/or sketch your ideas for solutions in the margins.

CLEANING UP

Alanna and Gus loved to ride their bikes to their local park. They swung on the swings, slid down the slide, and had picnics under the big tree. One day, as they set up their picnic, they noticed that there was trash in their way.

"Wow," said Gus, "look at all this junk." Where they usually sat for their picnic, they saw candy wrappers, empty juice boxes and yogurt containers, and plastic spoons.

"Looks like some other kids were eating here. Why did they leave all this trash here instead of putting it in the trash can?" wondered Alanna. Gus and Alanna always threw away their trash when they finished their picnics. There was a trash can on the other side of the park.

As they looked around, they noticed trash all around the park. It made them sad and mad. "It's time to clean up!" exclaimed Gus.

They went home and grabbed supplies. Gus brought some trash bags, and Alanna had two pairs of rubber gloves that her dad used to do the dishes. As they passed by Mrs. Jones's house, they noticed that she was trimming her trees. Gus had an idea.

"Hi, Mrs. Jones!" he called. "Would you mind if we took a couple of these branches?"

"Not at all," she replied. "What are you two up to today?"

"We're going to clean up the park," answered Alanna. "But what do we need branches for, Gus?"

"We can use them to pick up some of the trash," he said. "We just stab it, like this..." He grabbed a fairly straight branch and jabbed it into the grass. "That way, we don't have to touch the really gross stuff."

When Gus and Alanna got to the park, they began picking up food wrappers and chip bags.

CLEANING UP

"Ugh," said Alanna, "all of this stuff would have been easy for them to put in a trash can."

Gus found a plastic water bottle and some soda cans under a bush. He said, "We should put the stuff we can recycle in a separate bag."

"Great idea!" said Alanna. She pulled a second trash bag from Gus's backpack.

They finished cleaning up the playground area and proudly looked over their work.

"What about the pond?" asked Gus.

When they got to the pond, they were surprised. Not only was there trash in it, but there was also a rainbow-colored film on the top of the water.

"Ewwww," said Alanna. "What is that?"

"I think it's pollution," said Gus. "The parking lot is up there." He pointed up a small hill next to the pond. "When it rains, all the oil from the street and parking lot washes into this pond."

"Can we clean it up?" asked Alanna.

"I don't know how," answered Gus.

They fished out the trash they could reach with their sticks. They saw a duck floating on the pond. They worried about it getting sick from the pollution.

As they carried their full trash bags back to where they parked their bikes, Alanna asked, "How can we keep people from making this mess all over again?"

"Good question," said Gus. "How about we make posters and hang them in the park?"

"Great idea!" said Alanna. "Maybe we should ask the city to put more trash cans in the park, too."

"Excellent idea," said Gus. "Now, let's finally have our picnic!"

STEP 1: PREPARE FOR THE CHALLENGE

Problem What problem will you solve?	**Challenge** What will you do?	**Criteria** What should the solution do to be successful?	**Constraints** What are the limits?
Pollution from the street and parking lot is washing into the pond when it rains.	Engineer a way to keep pollution from getting into the pond.	The pollution barrier should keep two spoonfuls of oily water out of the pond area, so the paper towel "pond" should stay completely dry.	• Use only the materials given. • The pollution barrier cannot be attached to the container.

1. Your goal is to keep polluted water away from your pond, so you'll need to test some materials to see how they are affected by water. Carefully pour a spoonful of water on each material and observe. What happens to the water? Record your observations and think about how you could use each material to solve this challenge.

Material	**Observations**	**How could we use this material?**

2. How could combining materials—using them together—help you in this challenge?

_____

_____

NAME: _____   DATE: _____

STEP 2: BRAINSTORM, PLAN, AND BUILD

1. Brainstorm design ideas for pollution barriers you can build that will meet the criteria and constraints. Sketch and write at least three ideas on the back of this page. Your pollution barrier should stretch from one side of the test container to the other.

2. Think about which design might perform best in testing. Draw a star by the design you will build. Why did you choose this idea?

   _____

   _____

   _____

3. Draw a diagram of your design here. Label all of the materials.

4. Describe how your pollution barrier will keep polluted water from getting to your pond.

   _____

   _____

   _____

5. Build your pollution barrier model!

STEP 3: TEST, IMPROVE, AND SHARE

1. Place your duck (toy) on a paper towel at one end of the test container. The paper towel represents the pond. Put up your pollution barrier across the middle of the test container. Carefully pour two spoonfuls of polluted water into the other end of the test container. Wait one minute. Did your paper towel get wet? Why do you think this happened?

_____

_____

_____

_____

_____

_____

2. Share your pollution barrier with classmates. How can you use their ideas to make it better?

_____

_____

_____

_____

_____

3. Keep testing and improving until your pollution barrier keeps the paper towel dry for one minute!

STEP 4: REFLECT

1. How does your pollution barrier keep water away from your pond?

2. How did your design work the first time you tested it?

3. How did you improve your design?

4. What was the hardest part about this challenge?

5. What have you learned from this challenge?

PLOT SUMMARY:

> The Great Snow War is on! Team Yeti and Team Snow Way build snow forts to protect their team flags and battle it out with hand-thrown snowballs and a snowball launcher.

SNOWBALL LAUNCHER CHALLENGE:

Problem — What problem will you solve?	Challenge — What will you do?	Criteria — What should the solution do to be successful?	Constraints — What are the limits?
Team Yeti needs a snowball launcher.	Build a launcher that can fling a snowball model.	• The snowball model should fly at least three feet. • The snowball model should knock over at least two cups in a cup tower.	• Use only the materials given. • Don't cross the launch line.

OTHER POSSIBLE PROBLEMS AND CHALLENGES:

Students can use the *Universal Challenge Pages* (pages 104–107) to create solutions to any of the problems below or problems they identify themselves.

Problem	Everyone's hands get numb when they make snowballs.
Possible Challenges	• Design a snowball maker. • Engineer better gloves or a way to keep hands warm.

Problem	Both snow forts only have one wall.
Possible Challenge	• Design and build a model of a better snow fort.

Problem	Team Yeti needs a way to defend against snowballs thrown by the Flinger into their fort.
Possible Challenge	• Design a roof or other defense for the Team Yeti fort.

MATERIALS:

Required: snowball models, which can be crumpled-up sheets of paper, cotton balls, pom-poms, or any other roundish, light objects; paper or plastic cups for targets; painter's or masking tape

Suggested: structural materials such as rulers, craft sticks, straws, aluminum cans, paper and plastic cups, paper towel and toilet paper rolls, plastic cutlery; flexible or springy materials such as rubber bands, balloons, binder clips; connecting materials such as glue, string, tape

PREPARATION:

Set up a testing station by measuring out a three-foot-long area and placing a strip of painter's or masking tape at each end. A long table or set of desks will be easiest for students to test on, but space on the floor will work. Designate one end as the launch line. At the opposite end, build a few simple towers of five upside-down cups—three on the bottom row and two on the top. (See diagram on page 100.)

LESSON PLAN:

1. Have students read the passage and discuss the problems they identified. Use these questions as prompts:

   - Have you ever played in the snow? What was it like?
   - What are some problems the kids had in this story? Did they solve any of them? How?

2. Introduce the Snowball Launcher Challenge by reading through the challenge pages together. Show students the available materials and review the criteria and constraints. Explain and/or demonstrate that they will place or hold their launchers behind the launch line and launch a snowball model toward a cup tower.

3. Give students time to prepare, brainstorm, plan, and build their snowball launchers. Circulate to observe and answer questions as students work on their solutions. Remind them to use the challenge pages to guide them as they work through the engineering design process. If students are having trouble coming up with workable ideas, encourage them to research catapults, trebuchets, slingshots, and other launchers.

4. When they are ready for testing, observe to ensure fair and equal testing conditions for each student or team.

5. Have students share their solutions with the class and get feedback from peers, then revise their designs and test again.

6. When students have completed the challenge, have them demonstrate and explain their snowball launchers to the class. If desired, you can have a competition to see which snowball launcher will throw a snowball model the farthest, or have a race to see which team can completely knock down all the cups in a tower.

7. Have students fill out the reflection page.

8. If time, allow students to choose their own problem and testing setup and use the *Universal Challenge Pages* (pages 104–107) to complete their challenge.

Directions: Read the passage and underline the problems the characters have to face. Write and/or sketch your ideas for solutions in the margins.

■ SNOW WAR ■

The first snowball hit and exploded into a cloud of powder. The Great Snow War was on! The first team to capture the other team's flag would win.

The Great Snow War usually lasted for days. Each morning, the players would come out dressed for battle. Snow boots, heavy jackets, scarves, hats, and gloves made up the uniforms. The teams spent part of the morning making snowballs. Each player had their own technique. Zena from Team Yeti scooped up a handful of snow and used her bare hands to form a ball. She said the warmth from her hands helped melt the outer layer so it would stick together when it refroze. Max from Team Snow Way started with a handmade snowball for the core, then he rolled it in fluffy snow to add layers and make it bigger. Each team made piles of snowballs in their fort. Even with gloves, everyone's hands got pretty numb.

Team Yeti had built their snow fort at the top of a small hill. First, they shoveled snow into a long, curved pile near the top of the hill. Then, they stomped all over it with their boots to squash the snow down tight. When they ran out of snow from inside the fort, they carried buckets up the hill from below. By the time they were done, the wall was four feet tall and stretched from one side of the hill to the other. They posted their blue flag inside their fort.

Team Snow Way had taken a different approach. Their snow fort was built on flat ground. They packed snow into big, plastic boxes. Then, they turned the boxes over and big snow bricks slid out. They stacked the snow bricks into a long, straight wall about six feet tall. They left a few bricks out to create open windows. Their red flag was safely flying, protected by their fort.

All of the Team Yeti members were expert snowball throwers. They crouched behind the wall of their fort

SNOW WAR

and then popped up and started throwing. They could fire a snowball directly into the open windows of Team Snow Way's fort. Throwing down toward Team Snow Way's fort from up on the hill helped.

Team Snow Way had a secret weapon: the Flinger. They built it from scrap wood they found in a team member's garage. It could throw a snowball clear across the field and into Team Yeti's fort. This gave Team Snow Way a tremendous advantage. Team Yeti really didn't have any defense to protect the top of their fort.

The battle raged on all morning. Team Snow Way launched dozens of snowballs with their Flinger. Team Yeti used the extra snow to make more snowballs and throw them back. By noon, both teams were tired and hungry. The flags were still safe in their snow forts. The teams called a time-out and everyone headed home for lunch. They would all be back soon enough to continue the Great Snow War.

STEP 1: PREPARE FOR THE CHALLENGE

Problem	Challenge	Criteria	Constraints
What problem will you solve?	What will you do?	What should the solution do to be successful?	What are the limits?
Team Yeti needs a snowball launcher.	Build a launcher that can fling a snowball model.	• The snowball model should fly at least three feet. • The snowball model should knock over at least two cups in a cup tower.	• Use only the materials given. • Don't cross the launch line.

1. Have you ever seen a device that launches or throws something through the air? Describe it.

   _____

   _____

2. Some kinds of launchers, like a catapult, sit on the ground. Others, like a slingshot, are handheld. Which do you think could fling something farther? Which do you think could fling something more accurately? Why?

   _____

   _____

3. Here is what your target cup tower will look like. Mark where you will aim for your snowball model to hit. Why did you choose this spot?

   _____

   _____

   _____

   _____

   _____

▬▬▬ STEP 2: BRAINSTORM, PLAN, AND BUILD ▬▬▬

1. Brainstorm design ideas for snowball launchers you can build that will meet the criteria and constraints. Sketch and write at least three ideas on the back of this page.

2. Think about which design might perform best in testing. Draw a star by the design you will build. Why did you choose this idea?

_____

_____

_____

3. Draw a diagram of your design here. Label all of the materials.

_____

4. Why do you think this design will knock down at least two cups in a tower?

_____

_____

_____

5. Build your snowball launcher!

STEP 3: TEST, IMPROVE, AND SHARE

1. Test your snowball launcher by launching a snowball model at the tower. Did your snowball launcher knock down at least two cups? If not, try a few more times. If it still doesn't knock down two cups, how could you improve it so it does? If you successfully knocked down two cups, how could you improve your launcher so it knocks down more cups?

_____

_____

_____

_____

2. Improve your snowball launcher and test it again. How did it do? Could you improve it some more?

_____

_____

_____

_____

3. Share your snowball launcher with classmates. How can you use their ideas to make it better?

_____

_____

_____

4. Keep testing and improving your snowball launcher!

SNOWBALL LAUNCHER CHALLENGE

DATE: _____

STEP 4: REFLECT

1. How did you design the first version of your snowball launcher?

2. How did you improve the design?

3. What was the hardest part about this challenge?

4. What have you learned from this challenge?

NAME: _____ DATE: _____

STEP 1: PREPARE FOR THE CHALLENGE

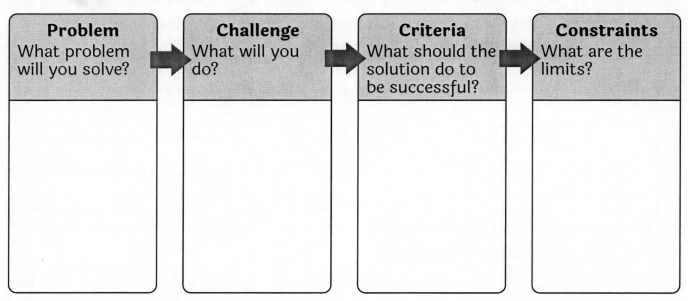

Problem What problem will you solve?	**Challenge** What will you do?	**Criteria** What should the solution do to be successful?	**Constraints** What are the limits?

1. Research similar real-world situations and solutions. Draw two examples below and write how you might use these ideas.

_____   _____

_____   _____

_____   _____

2. What do you need to know about the available materials? How can you test them to see how well they will help you solve the challenge?

_____

_____

_____

NAME: _____   DATE: _____

STEP 2: BRAINSTORM, PLAN, AND BUILD

1. Brainstorm design ideas for solutions to the challenge. Sketch and write at least three design ideas on the back of this page.

2. Think about which design might work best. Draw a star by the design you will build. Why did you choose this idea?

_____

_____

_____

3. Draw a diagram of your design here. Label all of the materials.

4. Describe how your solution will work.

_____

_____

_____

5. Build your solution according to your plan!

NAME: _____ DATE: _____

STEP 3: TEST, IMPROVE, AND SHARE

1. How will you test your solution?

_____

_____

_____

2. Test your solution. Was it successful? Why or why not?

_____

_____

_____

3. What can you do to improve your solution?

_____

_____

_____

4. Share your solution with friends. How can you use their ideas to make it better?

_____

_____

_____

5. Keep redesigning until your solution meets the criteria!

NAME: _____   DATE: _____

STEP 4: REFLECT

1. Describe how your design meets the criteria and constraints.

2. How did your design work the first time you tested it?

3. How did you improve your design?

4. What was the hardest part about this challenge?

5. What have you learned from this challenge?

MATERIALS LIST

It may help students to think of materials according to their possible function—extender, connector, controller, or mover—as defined in the chart below.

Extenders	Connectors	Controllers	Movers
can be used to create structure or add length	can be used to fasten things together	can be used to carry, confine, guide, or control something	can roll, float, spin, or otherwise move
craft sticks	glue and glue sticks	boxes	marbles
toothpicks	tape (clear, painter's, masking)	cans	Ping-Pong balls
cotton balls	rubber bands	plastic bottles	tennis balls
straws	pipe cleaners	paper or plastic cups, bowls, plates	racquetballs
unsharpened pencils	straws	cupcake liners	bouncy balls
rulers and yardsticks	string	cardboard tubes	plastic bottles
cardboard	yarn	milk cartons	cups
index cards	ribbon	cereal boxes	coins
playing cards	paper clips	plastic bags	metal washers
cardboard tubes	binder clips	bottle caps	nuts and bolts
egg cartons	stapler	balloons	packing peanuts
plastic cutlery	stickers or mailing labels	spoons	pom-poms
paper or plastic cups, bowls, plates	sticky notes	envelopes	cotton balls
plastic bottles	play clay	lunch sacks	marshmallows
lids	marshmallows, gumdrops, or apple chunks	gift bags	hard candies
polystyrene pieces	aluminum foil	trash bags	feathers
pipe cleaners	plastic wrap	egg cartons	toilet paper
dry spaghetti	toothpicks	plastic fruit baskets	tissues
blocks	twist ties		fabric
books			old CDs
math manipulatives			corks
			cardboard tubes

You'll notice that some materials appear in more than one category. Plastic cups make great controllers, but you can also build tall towers with them. Paper, depending on how it is cut or folded, could be used as an extender, a connector, a controller, or a mover. These categories are just a starting point—materials can be used in many other ways; for example, they can be wrapped around other materials or added for extra weight. Encourage students to think of multiple ways to use each material and to combine materials to create new uses.

PRICE SHEET

The budget is _____.

Challenge:

Item	Price
Total Spending:	

BUDGET SHEET

Directions:

1. List the name of your challenge at the top of the chart.
2. List each item that you will be using and its price.
3. Total your spending in the last row of each chart and then at the bottom of the page.

Total budget for this challenge:

_____

Challenge:

Original Plan			
Item	**Price**	**How Many?**	**Total**
		X	
		X	
		X	
		X	
		X	
		How much did we spend?	

Budget: _____

Spent: − _____

Left to spend: _____

Improved Plan			
Item	**Price**	**How Many?**	**Total**
		X	
		X	
		X	
		X	
		X	
		How much did we spend?	

Amount spent on original plan: _____

Amount spent on improved plan: + _____

Total amount spent: _____

Did you complete the challenge within the budget?

Yes   No

BOOKS WITH STEM PROBLEMS

Title and Author	STEM Problems
Charlotte's Web by E.B. White	• Construct a web to send a message. • Design baby spider parachutes.
Escape from Mr. Lemoncello's Library or *Mr. Lemoncello's Library Olympics* by Chris Grabenstein	• Design and build a board game. • Engineer a solar oven. • Design a better paper airplane.
Mr. Ferris and His Wheel by Kathryn Gibbs Davis	• Build a Ferris wheel model. • Design carnival rides.
The Calder Game by Blue Balliett	• Create a model of a maze with symbols. • Build a balanced kinetic sculpture.
The Cardboard Kingdom by Chad Sell	• Design a robot arm. • Engineer full-sized cardboard furniture.
The Misadventures of the Family Fletcher by Dana Alison Levy	• Engineer a way to keep balls and other sports equipment from going into the neighbor's yard. • Design a safe, humane skunk trap.
The Secret Science Alliance and the Copycat Crook by Eleanor Davis	• Invent something to help you sneak out of the house undetected. • Engineer a new mode of personal transportation. • Design a safe but annoying prank.
Twenty-One Elephants and Still Standing by April Jones Prince or *Twenty-One Elephants* by Phil Bildner	• Design and build different types of bridges. • Test bridges by placing weights on them.

BOOKS ABOUT ENGINEERS AND ENGINEERING

Title	Author
Calling All Minds: How to Think and Create Like an Inventor	Temple Grandin
Crazy Contraptions: Build Rube Goldberg Machines That Swoop, Spin, Stack, and Swivel	Laura Perdew
Engineer Academy: Are You Ready for the Challenge?	Steve Martin
How to Be an Engineer (Careers for Kids)	Carol Vorderman
Mistakes That Worked: 40 Familiar Inventions & How They Came to Be	Charlotte Foltz Jones
Out of the Box: 25 Cardboard Engineering Projects for Makers	Jemma Westing
Rube Goldberg's Simple Normal Humdrum School Day	Jennifer George
Secret Engineer: How Emily Roebling Built the Brooklyn Bridge	Rachel Dougherty
The Boy Who Harnessed the Wind	William Kamkwamba and Bryan Mealer
The Future Architect's Handbook	Barbara Beck
Who Built That? Bridges: An Introduction to Ten Great Bridges and Their Designers	Didier Cornille
Whoosh! Lonnie Johnson's Super-Soaking Stream of Inventions	Chris Barton